MW01171043

Forsaking Babylon

Handwritings to my Children

We would have healed Babylon, but she was not healed. Forsake her, and let us go each to his own country, for her judgment has reached up to heaven and has been lifted up even to the skies.

Jeremiah 51:9

KURT BORNE

All Bible verses taken from the English Standard Version (ESV).

The letters in this book were not written on the dates provided; however, they
accurately reflect all the events and thoughts of the author from those times.

Printed in the United States of America

Cover design by Jeanly Fresh Zamora

Author photography by Tracy Sgroi Mark Photography

Published by: Barefoot Publishing

Look for Kurt on Substack or contact him at:

forsakingbabylon@substack.com.

Table of Contents

To my children.

Hold these words close to your hearts, then
share them with your own children.

PREFACE

September 2022

Bubba and Sissy,

As you both know personally and painfully, life is hard. And I'm sure that I only know a portion of the pain you have felt thus far in your young lives. But trust me, for every day that I've known either of you was suffering, my heart broke. Between the two of you, my heart has broken many times over the years.

Life is indeed hard. It is hard in the day-to-day and week-to-week grind, but it is also hard because, well, it is simply hard to figure out. It is hard to figure out how to live, what to live for, why to even get out of bed in the morning.

Like most decent dads I have shared a number of valuable nuggets of wisdom about life with you over the years. And yet, I never adequately shared how those nuggets revealed themselves to me in my own life. Moreover, I have held back some even deeper insights that you can only now, as young adults, fully appreciate. You are old enough to understand the full picture of the wisdom I've learned, and how I learned it.

It took me many, many years to understand the truth, to find the answers to some of life's most challenging questions: What should I live for? How should I live? What is truth? What is my purpose here on Earth?

Many times, I thought I knew some of those answers, and many times I was wrong. Sometimes I had inklings of the right answers, but they quickly faded away. Other times, I thought I had it all figured out, and that the answers to life were obvious and logical, only to realize that I'd been misled, or I was misleading myself.

After many years of searching, the truth came to me. After many hard lessons and a few very insightful experiences, I finally did figure out what life is all about. You may be surprised to learn that the answers are fairly simple. But I want you to hear my stories so that you will feel the full impact of what I learned.

At some very pivotal moments in my life, I made a point of writing down the valuable lessons I was learning along the way. I pray that you take the following words, stories, and letters to heart. My hope is that you can learn what took me nearly 50 years to figure out about the true way to live. Your life, and more importantly your eternal life, very much depend on it.

For the time is coming when people will not endure sound teaching, but having itching ears they will accumulate for themselves teachers to suit their own passions, and will turn away from listening to the truth and wander off into myths.

2 Timothy 4:3-4

INTRODUCTION

September 2022

Kids,

The following Bible story encapsulates much of my young, naïve, and self-centered life. For most of my life I acted like a king, the king of my own little universe. I was only focused on myself, and that was my biggest problem. This Bible story comes from chapter 5 of the Book of Daniel. I paraphrase much of it here.

Belshazzar, King of Babylon, once held a great feast for a thousand of his lords. They dined on the most exquisite food and consumed the most exceptional wine from around the world.

Now, Belshazzar was not a very caring or generous king. In fact, he lived very selfishly, and self-centeredness was his custom. Everything was always about him, especially when it came to pleasing himself over others. He only craved for himself, and he only thought about himself.

And this King Belshazzar was cruel. He openly mocked anyone in his kingdom who dared to worship other gods above him, especially the Jewish people, who worshipped the one true God. He mocked not only by his words, but by his deeds. In fact, it was during this very feast that King Belshazzar took the sacred chalices of gold and silver from the Jewish people's temple—the house of God in Jerusalem—and he, his guests, and his many mistresses drank from those sacred chalices. On this night they drank wine and honored the king as well as their many false gods of gold, silver, iron, and stone, instead of worshipping the one true God.

But as they were celebrating, a very strange thing happened. The fingers of a human hand appeared out of nowhere and wrote on the wall of the king's palace, right in front of the king. King Belshazzar saw the hand as it wrote. He turned pale with fright, his knees buckled, and frightening thoughts started running through his mind, as he wondered about the meaning of such a mysterious sight.

The king immediately brought in his enchanters and astrologers in hopes that they could interpret the meaning of the mysterious writings on the wall. But none could interpret them.

Eventually the king called for the prophet Daniel, to see if he could interpret the handwriting on the wall. Daniel was a man of God, the same God that King Belshazzar was mocking that very night.

Daniel was able to interpret the writing on the wall. He told King Belshazzar that the strange words inscribed on the wall—Mene, Mene, Tekel, and Parsin—contained an ominous meaning.

"What does it mean?" the king insisted.

Daniel replied, "You, King Belshazzar, have not humbled your heart toward God in the way you live, even though you knew the truth about the one true God."

Daniel continued, *"But you have lifted up yourself against the Lord of heaven. And the vessels of his house have been brought in before you, and you and your lords, your wives, and your concubines have drunk wine from them. And you have praised the gods of silver and gold, of bronze, iron, wood, and stone, which do not see or hear or know, but the God in whose hand is your breath, and whose are all your ways, you have not honored." (Daniel 5:23)*

Then Daniel shared the ominous meaning of the writing on the wall. "The meaning of the words Mene, Mene, Tekel, and Parsin translate to this: God has numbered the days of your kingdom and is bringing it to an end. You have been weighed in the balances and have been found lacking. Your kingdom will therefore be divided and given to new earthly kings."

That very night King Belshazzar was killed as an invading army destroyed Babylon. This is documented not only in the Bible but in other historical records.

The irony is that the name Belshazzar means, "The gods protect the king." I guess the one true God didn't agree.

Kids, this book, this collection of letters, are my own warnings to you, in a sense. These are my warnings for how to avoid living in a Babylonian world—which our country has essentially been for many decades now—and instead walk the narrow path with God. We live in a world, in a country, in a society that worships the false gods of money, *stuff*, fame, social status, and more recently, *living your best life now.*

Even most Christians live this way, sadly. They say that they worship the one true God, but their actions prove otherwise. They too worship the ever-changing false gods that this world offers. They say the one thing, but do the other.

Throughout history and especially throughout the Holy Bible,

Babylon was regarded as a city filled with all the material wealth one could imagine, where the citizens seemingly had it all.

Our modern world includes many large and small Babylons, even millions of personal Babylons, where people have it all, yet they still crave more. We are a world that worships the many false gods surrounding us, even though we know about the one true God. Most all of modern society knows the truth about the one true God, but far too many choose to ignore that truth and instead pursue the here and now.

And so, we see a bunch of little kings and queens of Babylon running around, living selfishly, craving only for themselves, and thinking only about themselves. Kings and queens who are obsessed with living their best life now by way of gain—more money, more fame, more social status, and more stuff.

Yet all these little kings and queens are being found lacking in the eyes of God.

They drank wine and praised the gods of gold and
silver, bronze, iron, wood, and stone.

Daniel 5:4

Wandering in Babylon

Thus says the Lord concerning this people: "They have loved to wander thus; they have not restrained their feet; therefore the Lord does not accept them; now he will remember their iniquity and punish their sins."

Jeremiah 14:10

DUDLEY ROAD
Coasting in Comfort

How long will you lie there, O sluggard?
When will you arise from your sleep?

Proverbs 6:9

August 1984

To the future me,

Everything was going swimmingly.

Up to this point my life has been very comfortable and blessed. But almost overnight I received the rude awakening that living like a child has come to an end. It has to, I suppose. I simply failed to plan for it. High school is over, this month I will turn 18, and real life is supposed to begin in mere days.

I thought everything was going swimmingly, but in truth I was only being lazy, or maybe, irresponsible. My life has been comfortable and blessed, but only because I've been living as if in a dream state. Like an innocent (nay, clueless) child smiling while in a deep slumber, dreaming of rainbows and fairies.

Yes, that fairly well describes my life up to this point. I'm not lazy, per se. I just never had to exert much effort in order for things to go my way. Everything came easy to me growing up on Dudley Road. I've been coasting in comfort from the day I was born until I graduated high school this summer.

I was born with a bit of a silver spoon in my mouth—at least, I suppose, when compared to the average American kid growing up in the '70s and '80s. Not that my parents dared to let my siblings and me realize that we were better off than most kids. Oh no. We wore the cheap brand of clothes growing up. You know, the kind that you had enough awareness of to be slightly embarrassed about. But we never lacked clothes. We never went on extravagant vacations, but we still got a summer vacation every year. Our parents helped us kids to buy our own clunky used car when we turned 16, but indeed, we still had our own wheels.

We weren't spoiled, but we certainly never lacked. We were raised not to feel like we were better off than the average American kids. Yet, better off we were.

School came easy enough for me as well, even as my parents put me through the rigorous Catholic schools. I survived those schools as a *B* student because the nuns and my parents forced me to be a B student. I could get the Bs easy enough. I could have gotten As, but why bother when getting Bs was easier, and no one bothered you when you did? Being a B student meant that the grown-ups were satisfied enough to leave you alone. I knew that, and so that's what I did. Easy.

Getting jobs was easy too. It was easy for me to earn just enough money to meet my youthful needs. At first, I only needed enough money to buy records and snacks, and the occasional trip to Putt-Putt Golf, and so that's all I earned. Upon reaching age 16, when I needed enough to pay for gas and car insurance, that's how much I earned. And barely a penny more. Easy.

I had plenty of structure and discipline growing up, which is a blessing that no one appreciates until years and decades later. That structure and discipline helped me to get things done—job, money, grades. However, I was also clever enough to use that discipline to do just the minimum required of me to get by. *Just enough* was my goal. The rest of my time was focused on socializing.

I made friends easily too, thanks to a dry, self-deprecating, and irreverent sense of humor. That sense of humor and decent looks even made it possible to come up with a few girlfriends without Herculean efforts.

In fact, it has been in the final couple of years of my youth—junior and senior years of high school—that my social life really took off. My circle of friends became wider and wider. It's gotten to the point where people want to come up and introduce themselves to me simply because they've heard so much about me. These are total strangers, some of them even cute girls! Can you imagine?

That kind of thing will go to your head. It could even lead to you becoming too comfortable.

I have friends from all walks of life: the honor students, the preppies, the student government types, the jocks, and the cheerleaders. I also get along great with the punk rockers and the stoners. Oddly enough, I was never considered part of any one of those groups; maybe that's why I can mingle among all of them.

And so, all up and down Dudley Road and throughout Northern

Kentucky I've been the king of my own little domain! Popularity and social status, comfort and ease, as far as my naïve eyes can see.

This has been my young life: structure and discipline, but no pressure, no stress, and getting all my simple desires met with complete ease. Add to that my explosion onto the social scene as an upperclassman. To say I've been coasting comfortably is an understatement.

The '80s are perfect for this easy living mindset. It's been easy to find fun and cheap entertainment here in the '80s. We seem to have everything: great music to either purchase or record off the radio, big fat movie theaters to go to, and the malls and fast-food joints to hang out in.

We even have MTV now, which is an awesome TV channel that shows nothing but music videos of rock and pop bands. You don't even have to make elaborate plans to have a party anymore, thanks to MTV. You simply call a few friends—who then call a few girls— to "meet at so-and-so's house to watch MTV on Friday night." Before you know it, you have a nice little party of 8-12 people. How great is that? Even our parties, these MTV parties, are easy and fun.

And if we want to do anything crazier than watching MTV, also easy! We just head up to the local McDonald's on Buttermilk Pike after about 8 p.m. Why McDonalds? Because that's where everyone meets to spread the word about who is having larger parties that night, maybe even *open parties* where anyone can show up.

I write all of this to emphasize the following revelation I've recently had.

So, through all this easy living, my childlike brain thinks, "This must be what life is all about. I'm certain of it. How could it not be?" My life has been comfortable and easy, every day, every year, from my childhood in the '70s to my teen years in the '80s.

Until graduation.

Until this cursed summer of 1984, the summer after high school graduation.

I've been swimming so effortlessly down my river of comfort and ease that I failed to realize that that stream had to eventually empty into the ocean of the real world. I've now been awakened from my slumber to see all my friends leaving for college, jobs, or both. Yet I have no plan because I've been too busy enjoying the easy life. I fell for an illogical belief that I could exist forever in this worldly comfort.

I wrongly believed that the answer to life was to, only and always, seek comfort and ease. Well, you idiot, that's easy to do when you are supported by your parents. But what happens when adulthood smacks you upside the head? I've been existing in a sort of coma, stuck living a lie about life's purpose.

I decided to write this down because I need to remember this moment. It is proving to be a hard lesson learned. I think I'll write down all such big moments in my life. If not for my own sake, maybe I can share what I'm learning with someone who needs to hear it.

I have a feeling that this is the first of many big lessons I'm going to learn.

Signing off,
Kurt

P.S. – It took this rude awakening to get me thinking for the first time about the meaning of life, what its purpose is, and what my own unique purpose is. So, despite the unenviable position I'm in,

I'm actually kind of excited to be thinking about these things—the meaning of life and my purpose in this world. Even though my starting point (right now) is admittedly a pretty low one, at least I feel awake finally. I learned a hard lesson, but I'm now alert.

And so, I have to decide what to do next. Yikes! Kind of scary but also kind of exciting. It's time to awaken from my slumber.

Go to the ant, O sluggard; consider her ways, and be wise.
Without having any chief, officer, or ruler, she prepares
her bread in summer and gathers her food in harvest.

Proverbs 6:6-8

5TH & VINE
Venturing Forth

Everyone who goes on ahead and does not abide in the
teaching of Christ, does not have God. Whoever abides
in the teaching has both the Father and the Son.

2 John 1:9

December 1984

Kids,

Yeah, so, I realized that rather than writing these letters to myself, I should instead write them with my future children in mind. So, whoever and however many of you are to come, I am dedicating and writing these letters to you, and to your children, and your children's children.

Well, I woke up from my rose-colored slumber at the end of the summer. I was rudely smacked in the face with the reality that my comfort and ease were quickly evaporating. I found myself at the doorstep of adulthood, of real life, and I had no plan. What was I to do?

One day I'm hosting one of the most historic graduation parties in Northern Kentucky, and the next day, everyone's gone. Everyone was heading off to adulthood except me. I was still holding a beer in one hand and a Frisbee in the other. That whole *coasting in comfort* plan wasn't cutting it anymore.

So, what to do next?

The only sensible thing to do, or so I thought, was to enroll in the local college where my mother works, and where I could therefore get free tuition. Adding to that, the most sensible way to pay my few bills was to live at home with my parents and go to work at my dad's company.

You can probably guess where this plan is heading.

It didn't take long—about two months—for me to realize I'd made yet another big life mistake. I tried to take the easy way out, and I was becoming more ashamed of myself by the week. I went from being jarred into reality from my happy high school slumber, to choosing a depressing existence of going into the family business and essentially living completely dependent on my parents.

It turns out that this thing called life is not going to be easy. I realized that a difficult conversation with myself had to take place. And so that's what I did. Some very deep soul searching took place over the next few weeks, this past fall. The result of that self-reflective period was me concluding, "What the heck, you only live once. So, let's go extreme."

And extreme for this local boy—who had never done anything rash or unexpected all his life—is to join the military.

Like probably so many men before me who'd found themselves in a similar bind—that of having no other logical life choice—I came up with this wild idea. I can't even remember how the idea first entered my head. I think I saw a recruitment commercial on TV, kinda like Bill Murray did in the recent movie *Stripes*. My family has no real military history, and none of my privileged Catholic friends were joining the military. I'm not really sure how I came up with such a crazy idea, but I'm glad for it all the same.

At any rate, this beats my first big decision by a mile, that first so-called life plan that fell flat within a couple of months. That first plan of going to the local college and working for daddy failed because, well, it wasn't so much a plan as a path of least resistance.

As it turns out, that first plan was both the worst and the best decision of my life. Let me explain. It was the worst decision because relying on one's parents as you enter adulthood is simply a terrible plan. It was the best decision, however, precisely because it was the worst decision. In other words, that decision was *so bad* that my reaction—upon realizing my folly—was to choose the opposite, something as nuts as joining the military.

And so that's what finds me sitting here at the Westin Hotel in downtown Cincinnati, at the corner of 5th and Vine streets. I'm sitting in the lounge having a couple of beers as I contemplate what lies ahead. I love coming here to look down on Fountain Square; it gives me a nostalgic feeling for my hometown. Plus the fact that they'll serve beer to an 18-year-old. Shhhh.

It's late December and I'm listening to *Do They Know It's Christmas?* for probably the hundredth time this month. It's kind of ironic now, hearing that Christmas song, which came out to raise awareness of the famine happening in Ethiopia. Between that song and joining the military, I've started waking up to the larger world around me. No more coasting in comfort in my own little universe, like I wrote about in my first letter.

Anyway, wow, what a momentous day for me! I just came from the local recruitment office nearby where I signed my life away, as they say. I signed the enlistment paperwork, I've sworn in, and I am set to head off next May *into the wild blue yonder* as the Air Force theme song goes. I'm only going to be doing a desk job, but that's not the point for me. The point is simply shaking up this sluggardly life and getting out of this rut that I'm in.

I must say that I am nervous about what the future holds, but I have an even greater feeling of excitement. I never would have thought that the *unknown* could hold such sway over me. I'm not too nervous about having to face actual military danger. Ronald Reagan recently won reelection, and it looks like he has things in control in terms of world affairs. (Actually, the Soviets and U.S. seem to be stuck in a staring contest, with no one willing to set off their nuclear weapons, and wisely so.)

I guess it will be kinda hard getting through bootcamp and leaving home for the first time on my own. But how hard can it really be? After all, it's been done by so many men before me. Like my friends and I often joke about things completely unknown, we say with a dismissive wave of the arm, "It'll be fine!"

Anyway, this whole decision-making process has been intriguing. I feel like this is the answer for me, the answer to that question, "How should one live their life?" I truly believe that, for me, the answer is adventure, the answer is to dive into the unknown and see what life has to offer. It sure feels like that's the answer, anyway. It truly feels awesome, exciting, and honestly, mind-blowing. It is by far the best feeling I've ever had in my life, so I think I've made the right decision.

I'll sign off for today. It's a strange thing to consider, what my next letter will be about. Because I have no clue what will happen between now and that next letter. I'm more determined now than ever to keep writing these letters to you kids.

Yes, adventure and the unknown may just be the answer to life. We will see.

Love,
Dad
(That sounds funny calling myself dad. I'm only 18 years old.)

P.S. – Even with all this exciting life change about to happen, there is one strange thing I must mention, although I can't exactly put my finger on it.

I have this unsettling feeling like I'm forgetting something. Like I'm about to take off into the unknown and forgetting something critical, something that I'm supposed to take with me. It's not a physical thing that I'm forgetting, though. Instead, it's more like a universal truth or reality that I need to have with me when I leave the comforts of home.

Or...you know what it is? It's like I'm supposed to take a best friend with me, but I forgot to buy them a plane ticket. I know that may sound dumb, but it's kinda like that.

Or, actually, here it is. I feel like I should somehow be able to take both a best friend and my dad with me, guys who will be there every moment to support me and give me good advice, and at the same time make me feel like I never truly left home.

Does that make any sense?

Maybe this feeling is merely me having second thoughts. Or me being a bit scared of what this exciting unknown holds for me, since I've never done something this unique before.

That would be amazing, though, if I could somehow leave home but also have my dad and a best friend go with me.

> *And if you forget the Lord your God and go after other*
> *gods and serve them and worship them, I solemnly*
> *warn you today that you shall surely perish.*
>
> *Deuteronomy 8:19*

SANTA CRUZ
Idolizing Fun

I said in my heart, "Come now, I will test you with pleasure;
enjoy yourself." But behold, this also was vanity.

Ecclesiastes 2:1

November 1986

Children,

Much has happened since I last wrote one of these letters. I've
already been in the Air Force for a year and a half, and it has been
a crazy adventure. Looking back at my last letter, I suppose that is
exactly what I wanted. Adventure, and lots of fun. It has been an
enormous success in that regard, but now I am starting to have my
doubts. But before I get to that, let me backtrack to the beginning
of my adventures.

I left that May of 1985 for bootcamp in San Antonio, Texas. As you
might expect, it was about the worst six weeks of my life. It wasn't
impossible, because even a guy like me who is really not suited for

that kind of thing, well, even I survived. At the end of the training, I went with a few guys to visit the San Antonio River Walk, which is a very cool submerged canal that runs through the downtown area. It's full of restaurants, bars, and shopping. It would have been more fun if we could have worn civilian clothes and had a few beers. But it was still pretty cool. Then I went to Biloxi, Mississippi for my job training. During that six-week period I got to hang out with some guys on a little island beach, and also spend a weekend in New Orleans. That was when I realized, "Okay now that bootcamp is over, I can start to have some real fun."

After all my training was finished, I got lucky and am currently stationed here in California, at Travis Air Force Base. Travis is in Northern California, which has turned out to be very cool. Since coming here, I've been able to visit San Francisco a bunch of times, Sacramento, Yosemite National Park, Monterrey, Santa Cruz, Berkeley, and Oakland. I even flew down to Las Vegas one weekend to hang out with my parents. I've seen a number of great concerts, ballgames, and done a bunch of crazy stuff in San Francisco. One weekend, stupid as this sounds, we spent an entire day driving around the hills of San Fran playing *Punch Bug*, for no particular reason other than that we were bored.

Needless to say, it has certainly been an adventure thus far, and it has been one fun thing after another. I fell in with a great group of guys here, and all we seem to do is figure out unique ways to have a blast. For example, for a while there we were making regular Thursday night trips to a certain nightclub on the campus of U.C. Davis. We simply act like idiots dancing and drinking, doing mischievous things around the bar and on the dance floor.

We've made weekend trips to Lake Tahoe, camped on the Rubicon River, taken road trips around the Bay Area and a few beach weekends on the Santa Cruz Beach Boardwalk. In fact, we just recently took a trip there, and boy was it a doozy.

That last trip to Santa Cruz felt like a culmination of the past year and a half of my fun and adventure. Lots of alcohol was consumed, lots of women chased, and somehow we even found ourselves taking some illicit drugs, which is probably the craziest thing I've ever done. Let's just say that those drugs resulted in something we famously call the Denny's Death March the next morning, as we completed a sort of magical mystery stroll to the nearby Denny's restaurant, desperate for food.

Now, I share all these things in a boastful way because it really was a ton of fun, and certainly an adventure. But I sit here today feeling kinda empty, unsatisfied, confused, and lost about it all. I throw in the feeling of *lost* because, perhaps not a complete coincidence, I heard that a teenage movie called *The Lost Boys* was being filmed this year right there on the Santa Cruz boardwalk. I don't know what the movie is about, exactly, because it hasn't come out yet. It's just ironic that that's how I feel right now, at this early point in my so-called adventurous life...like some kind of lost boy. Maybe lots of military guys feel this way, seeking fun and adventure while also feeling alone.

Part of this feeling may stem from the fact that a number of the guys are starting to move on. A couple of them got transfer orders to other bases, and other guys are wandering away to their girlfriends or other things. It's a *breaking up the band* kind of feeling, I suppose.

I think my feeling of being lost goes much deeper than having my group of friends break up, however. I'm starting to think there's more to life than purely seeking out as many versions of fun and adventure as I can imagine. Certainly, the fun times are fun, even spectacular and exhilarating while they are happening, while I am in the moment. But then I always, inevitably, have to go back to my boring Air Force job on Monday morning.

I'm starting to see that while I love having the fun on the weekends, that those are merely the high points in between even more days of low points. Is this what adult life is like? At least in our world today, most adults seem like they trudge along in jobs they don't like, solely to survive until Friday when they can let loose. And that's how the guys and I have been living.

The fun only comes in small spurts. Life is too much of a roller coaster when it is lived like that. There are too many low points—boring job + being home sick during the week—that take away from the less frequent high points. I guess I would have to be independently wealthy to be able to have fun all the time. But I don't see that happening anytime soon.

So, while seeking out fun and adventure as the answer appears great, part of me thinks that that can't possibly be the complete answer. Fun can't be sustained 24 hours a day, 365 days a year. Not to mention there is often a feeling of a letdown after each fun adventure. That's probably because as each bit of fun ends, it is merely a reminder that fun can't last forever.

I'm not sure what I'll do now, in terms of finding life's answers. I guess I have to continue on my quest.

Perhaps I'll try to get a transfer somewhere else like a few of my buddies did. But where else would be as fun as California? Maybe overseas. Yes, that might be cool. We'll see.

Well kids, I look forward to having something interesting to write to you next time. And I hope to be closer to finding the answers to life.

Until then,
Dad

P.S. – I hope you don't read these letters someday and realize that they are nothing more than the youthful ramblings of your dad. Rather, I hope that they point you in a positive direction. Like in this letter, I hope you'll learn that striving for fun all the time isn't a realistic goal in life. It can't truly be achieved, I am learning.

One thing I am learning is that the answer to life, and my purpose in it, will have to be something that can sustain me every day. That can't be attained through just partying and fun. The answer to life, if it is the big deal that I believe it is, will surely be something that fulfills my every day, every week, every year, every moment.

Anyway, I hope that in the totality of all the letters I write, when put together, will tell a good story for you kids about how to live life. I just hope I can find the answers myself first.

> *They have lyre and harp, tambourine and flute and wine at their feasts, but they do not regard the deeds of the Lord, or see the work of his hands.*

> *Isaiah 5:12*

AMSTERDAM
Parading the World

*"But watch yourselves lest your hearts be weighed down
with dissipation and drunkenness and cares of this life,
and that day come upon you suddenly like a trap."*

Luke 21:34

April 1988

Kiddos,

Kiddos, ha ha, that's what my dad calls my siblings and me. Speaking of my dad, I'm really missing him right now, as well as my mom, my whole family and everybody back home, for that matter. I've been away almost a full year, stationed in Western Europe.

I can't believe I let an entire year go by without writing one of these letters. I guess I got distracted by the change of scenery.

Where to begin?

So right after I ended that last letter, I did in fact put in for a transfer to various places in Europe, and I lucked out and got orders to go to an air base near the small town of Florennes, in Belgium. I didn't know much of anything about Belgium at the time, but I was pretty excited once I saw how central it is to a lot of very cool places.

I've been stationed here for a one-year tour, which is about to end. I'm glad to be getting out of here soon, as I am pretty homesick. This is my first time having travelled outside the U.S., and while feeling homesick, it has truly been an amazing experience.

The reason for me being here itself is pretty fascinating. Hopefully you'll learn about this in school, but we are currently involved in something called the Cold War with the Soviet Union. The Cold War isn't a war in the typical sense. Basically, we and our allies are going face to face against the Soviet Union and its allies. In a nutshell, we are both threatening each other with nuclear war; but because both sides know that if the other side *pulls the trigger,* it will be the end of everyone, literally. So no one dares to pull that trigger. And therefore, both sides simply keep building more weapons to point at each other. When I write it on paper it sounds pretty juvenile, honestly.

I believe our strategy is that we're trying to bankrupt the Soviets, because we believe that we can afford to keep building up arms, but that they can't. The hope is that we can bankrupt them and we'll win by default.

Who knows when this Cold War will end, though; it's been going on since the end of World War II (more than 40 years already). I'm going to go out on a limb and predict that it will be over long before you kids are born. I think our plan of outspending the Soviets might honestly work. Not to mention the fact that the current Soviet leader, Mikhail Gorbachev, actually seems to have some common sense in realizing that communism doesn't work (it's never worked). Our hope is that the Soviet leader wants to focus on his people's and his country's well-being more than solely trying to win this Cold War. At least that is my hope.

A lot of terrible things have come out about the Soviet Union in recent decades, possibly worse than what Hitler did to the Jewish people in World War II, if you can believe that. Most recently, only a year before I arrived here (in 1986), there was a significant nuclear accident at a place called the Chernobyl Nuclear Power Plant, which is in the Soviet Union. The Soviet government hid the truth about the disaster from its people and from the entire world, even while potential nuclear fallout was literally floating over Europe. How crazy! From all that I've learned, it appears that no truth exists with Soviet communism. It may be decades before the truth comes out about the damage done at Chernobyl and how many people died there.

Anyway, I trust you'll learn about much of this—the Cold War, Chernobyl, and the Soviet Union—when you go to school. It truly is intriguing, the complex history of Europe, Russia, and honestly the history of the entire world. Intriguing in how nations and wars affect each other over the years, decades, and centuries. A lot of death and misery and power and conquest have dominated world history.

During my year in Europe, I've learned a lot about its many very dark histories. I've taken a number of guided tours around Western Europe, and I've discovered some pretty dark stuff. I visited Dachau, which was one of the German concentration camps during World War II. I saw the ovens that the Nazi guards used to burn Jewish bodies. I also visited lots of beautiful cathedrals in the region, only to learn that, in my opinion, they were built essentially by slave labor.

I've visited several monuments built to commemorate bloody battles in just this tiny region of Belgium, Luxembourg, and France. For example, the Battle of Waterloo, where tens of thousands died in 1815, sits just 75 miles away from where many more tens of thousands perished at the Battle of the Bulge 130 years later. In between those battles, during World War I and only 85 miles away, the Battle of Verdun took hundreds of thousands of lives. And yet, all those numbers will seem miniscule when I tell you that more than three million soldiers died at the nearby site of the Western Front during World War I.

Lots and lots of lives lost throughout Europe, that's for sure, often to satisfy the egos of men who fancied themselves as gods. Men like Napoleon and Hitler, trying to control as much of their worlds as possible. I suppose that such men were their own answer to the meaning of life. Inexplicable, tragic, and sad.

Well, I spent more time writing about those topics than I intended. My intent was to put in perspective the reason for me being here. Why does the United States Air Force have an air base in Belgium, in other words? To that point, the primary function of our little air base is to keep ground-launched cruise missiles (GLCMs)—or as we call them, *glicoms*—ready to fire at East Germany and other Soviet Bloc nations. (I'm pretty certain these things could reach all the way to Moscow, however.) So we have a whole base full of people supporting the aiming of missiles at our enemy. And yet everyone's desperate prayer is that we never have to fire these same missiles. Because to do so means the end. Pretty sad and terrifying all at once.

Oddly, my friends, me, and everyone else here is able to compartmentalize that terrifying reality and still enjoy ourselves in our time off. The psychology of human beings is amazing, I am learning.

Anyway, I've been able to see and experience many crazy and wonderful things in only a year's time, and not solely historical tours of the dark side of Europe. I visited Paris a couple of times, seeing the Notre Dame Cathedral, Eiffel Tower, and the Palace of Versailles. In West Germany I got to experience Neuschwanstein Castle and Oktoberfest in Munich. I often visited the nearby cities of Bruges and Brussels here in Belgium, and more faraway places like England, Austria, Luxembourg, and Switzerland. And I went up to Amsterdam in the Netherlands a few times.

Lots of crazy, unique experiences at every turn, it seems, especially in Amsterdam. That city has a reputation for being wild, but my experiences weren't so much wild as just plain weird. In fact, I recently went back there one last time with a couple of buddies, to see what kind of trouble we could get ourselves into. As the *dumb Americans*, that wasn't hard to accomplish. Somehow, we managed to spend several hours—from happy hour leading into the evening—in a lesbian bar. The kind ladies played along, knowing we were clueless young Americans. But it was all in fun, and one of many stories to tell back home.

I sure have loved my year overseas; it really makes life super interesting. I know that none of my friends back home have experienced anything like this.

Now, all that being said, kids, I must admit that I'm not any closer to discovering the truth about how to live a life. Ahhhhhh! This is frustrating. It doesn't make sense. I'm probably at the greatest peak I can imagine, mixing fun with international experiences, and yet I simply don't feel as fulfilled as I thought I would be.

It's kinda the same as I described in my last letter, that the fun and experiences come in spurts, and that there's no way to sustain them through my weeks and months. For every peak, there is a valley. Yes, the peaks are fantastic, but they are few and far between. My amazing European road trips have about a month of boring days in between.

There is something else that's bothering me, but I'm not sure I can explain it properly. Since leaving home, and especially after this year in Europe, my world has gotten much bigger, more complex, and more full of experiences. But the bigger and more full of experiences it gets, my world get equally more confusing. It's like the more I experience, the more cluttered my brain gets.

I feel like all this *living* clouds my thinking, in terms of being able to discover my purpose and the meaning of life. I guess what I'm saying, kids, is that I am no closer to discovering the meaning of life, or my place in it, and it only appears to be getting more difficult to find.

So, my journey continues.

I'm leaving Europe soon to go back to the states. I have one more year in the Air Force, and then I am getting out. My next station is in boring Central Illinois. I plan to simply get through that final year and then get out of the service. At that time, I think I'll be ready to finish college somewhere. Maybe getting a formal education will help me figure this thing out about life.

I will close by telling you that while international travel certainly does give you wild experiences and lots of fun, that alone cannot be the answer to how to live life.

Love,
Dad

P.S. – It occurred to me that as sad as Europe's bloody history is, also sad is that in my quest to see the world, I've allowed myself to become a pawn in just another of the world's militaries taking up residence here. While I traversed this continent, I did so as simply one more soldier, walking among the ghosts of so many soldiers before me.

When viewed in that context, I realize that discovering truth and the answers to life is a great deal more profound, and more complicated, than globetrotting as some kind of tourist. Discovering the meaning of life is—and should be treated as—a vast ethical, moral, and philosophical undertaking. It is certainly not a task to be trifled with.

If I'm going to continue this search for truth, for the meaning of life, I need to do so more reverently.

> *For my thoughts are not your thoughts, neither are your ways my ways, declares the Lord. For as the heavens are higher than the earth, so are my ways higher than your ways and my thoughts than your thoughts.*

> *Isaiah 55:8-9*

ALTER HALL
Seeking Wisdom

Trust in the Lord with all your heart, and do not lean on your own understanding. In all your ways acknowledge him, and he will make straight your paths. Be not wise in your own eyes; fear the Lord, and turn away from evil.

Proverbs 3:5-7

December 1991

Hey kids,

It's been a few years since I last wrote to you. Much has happened since, and much more is about to take place in my life.

As I ended my last letter I had about one year left in my Air Force enlistment. My final months spent in Central Illinois were so uneventful that they are not worth mentioning. But right after my discharge, I enrolled at Xavier University in the summer of 1989. I decided that my best course of action, post-military, was to use the G.I. Bill to finish my bachelor's degree.

I chose Xavier because I knew it had a strong academic reputation. It also holds a bit of nostalgia for me since my dad and uncle both went there. And because it's in my hometown, it allowed me to finish school and save money by living with my parents. (But don't worry, I have a plan that ensures I won't be staying with my parents much longer. More about that in a moment.)

I had taken a number of college classes while in the Air Force, so I only needed two and a half years at Xavier to finish my degree. I finished my last final exams a few days ago, but I won't actually go through the graduation ceremony until next May. I couldn't be more content and relieved with having achieved this milestone. Getting four years of college courses completed isn't easy, that's for sure. I must say, though, that these past couple of years at Xavier have, in a way, been even more rewarding than my time in the service, including going overseas.

I guess until you are in the right mindset, you can't fully appreciate higher learning for what it is, or what it can be. Maybe not everyone has as rewarding an experience as I did. But for me, these past couple of years were extremely enriching. As I was going through it all, I really felt like I had found the answer to life's purpose, in a manner of speaking. That purpose being to gain deeper knowledge, or wisdom, about the world around me.

I must admit I was in a type of cocoon during my time at Xavier. I've been working a third shift job at the Cincinnati International Airport, sorting boxes for DHL Airways. By working such an odd schedule, and going to school, I rarely even saw my parents. So it felt like I was doing all this deep learning in solitude, which honestly made the experience all the more rewarding. Add to that the fact that Xavier, being a Jesuit liberal arts college, requires students to take a wide range of courses in language, English, history, theology, and philosophy.

Most of my classes were held in Alter Hall on Xavier's small campus. It is ironic that I had such a rich experience in such an absolutely nondescript building as Alter Hall. Looking at the building you would think it was a drab administrative building out of the Soviet Union. But it is there that I learned so, so much. That ugly building will forever hold a special place in my memory.

These past few years have been pretty odd. My school semesters were spent buried in books, living as a night owl, and passing what little free time I had with a few select friends. But it was such a wonderful experience to live like that for a couple of years.

My history, philosophy, and theology courses opened my eyes even further to the rest of the world, to all of humanity, it feels. I even read a number of books that were not required, which is funny because I used to hate reading. I've especially fallen in love with English literature classics and Russian novels, of all things. My favorites are *The Death of Ivan Ilyich, Death of a Salesman, 1984, We, Babbitt, Walden,* and *The Brothers Karamazov.* I love these books and others like them because they address the very question I have been trying to answer, which is how best to live and what to live for.

These past couple of years also added to my interest in history, and how history ties into religion and human psychology. The course that blew my mind was a course titled "The Holocaust" that was taught by a Jewish rabbi. That course alone was life altering.

Speaking of history, my goodness, I feel like I'm living during some of the biggest events in world history right now. For example, just as I alluded to in my last letter, communism did indeed fall around the world. A great song came out this year called "Right Here, Right Now" by a band called Jesus Jones. The song is about watching history in the making, as we watched the Berlin Wall come tumbling down and the Soviet Union giving up on communism. Absolutely crazy.

And during the same timeframe, we literally watched an actual war take place on TV. My parents had recently gotten cable TV, and we watched the Persian Gulf War take place, live, between the U.S. and Iraq. It was so strange, like watching a live documentary.

Between the amazing education I was getting, and seeing these big global events taking place, the past few years have been both surreal and supremely satisfying. To my original point for starting these letters, maybe seeking knowledge and truth is the ultimate answer. Maybe.

But—and you probably guessed there would be a *but*—I still haven't found what I'm looking for. As strongly as I feel that seeking knowledge and truth is the answer to life, I must admit that it can't be the full answer. Why? Because I still have this feeling of not being completely fulfilled. Constant *seeking* without ever fully *finding* can't be the end all, be all, I don't think.

Just like I felt about partying and living overseas, gaining wisdom and knowledge is wonderful, but they don't completely fill the void of my questions. Worldly knowledge has put a lot of my life and the world around me into great perspective, but it hasn't fully answered my ultimate question. What is the meaning of my life? What is my purpose? My God, kids, I frankly can't seem to get to the answer!

I need to keep searching, but at least now I know that reading and learning are definitely going to help me get there. Experiencing life, like I was doing in the Air Force, is also important to answering my questions. But awesome life experiences and the endless pursuit of knowledge and wisdom alone are not the meaning of life.

And with that, I can tell you what my next big plan is. This sounds weird, I'm sure, since only a couple of years ago I got out of the military. But I have decided to next join the Peace Corps. The Peace Corps is an organization started in the 1960s by President Kennedy, whereby U.S. citizens go to various nations around the world to volunteer their time in various development projects.

I got the idea from an old high school buddy of mine who returned this year from his own two years with the Peace Corps, spent in Thailand. Since I was nearing graduation at Xavier and still didn't know what I wanted to do with my life, I thought, "What the heck, let's do another adventure."

Maybe the answer to my questions is in another part of the world.

So I started looking into the Peace Corps, got ahold of their literature, and filled out an application. As an economics major, and having taken two years of Spanish classes, I signed up for an economics-related job in Spanish-speaking countries. In no time at all, the Peace Corps responded and offered me a volunteer position in Paraguay, South America.

I am scheduled to take off at the end of May, shortly after my graduation ceremony at Xavier. My Peace Corps job will have something to do with helping a local credit union to establish a home improvement loan program. I'm not totally clear on what that entails, but I will know soon enough.

Needless to say, my next letter or letters should be pretty interesting.

Love,
Dad

P.S. – Kids, I'll admit a feeling that I'm having, which is that I'm kinda nervous inside about leaving for the Peace Corps, even as exciting as it sounds. When I left for the Air Force I was nervous, but that's because I had never left home before. You wouldn't think

I'd be nervous now, since I've done this kind of thing already with the military.

Perhaps it's because the environments are so different. In the military I always had Americans around me, people with similar backgrounds. The Peace Corps isn't going to be like that at all. As soon as my training is finished, I'll be virtually on my own in a town that they assign me to—for two years. And I may be the only English-speaking person, and the only American, within miles of where I live. I guess we'll see, but this is certainly going to test my inner resolve.

I think doing something to this extreme level is what's going to be required of me to find the answers to life's big questions. So far, I've learned quite a few good lessons about what the answers to life are *not*. They are not found in living a life of comfort and ease. They are not found in a life of fun, partying, and international travel. They are not even found in seeking endless wisdom through higher education and consuming books.

My gosh, do I actually need to go to a third world country to discover the answers to life?

Apparently so.

For in much wisdom is much vexation, and he
who increases knowledge increases sorrow.

Ecclesiastes 1:18

PIRIBEBUY
Discovering Another

An excellent wife who can find? She is far more precious than jewels. The heart of her husband trusts in her, and he will have no lack of gain.

Proverbs 31:10-11

May 1993

Children,

I first saw your mother on a street somewhere in the middle of Miami. She was part of the same group of volunteers with me, preparing to fly off to Paraguay to serve in the Peace Corps for two years. Miami was a blur—a mere couple of days of processing, getting immunized, and going to briefings—before 40 of us flew off to South America. The only thing that sticks out in my mind is that single moment I saw her through a crowd. It wasn't love at first sight, but more like *intense interest at first sight*.

Realizing that she was in the same group of volunteers as me, I knew that I'd have time later to get to know her. Well, later came halfway to Paraguay. We were on a lengthy layover in Sao Paulo, Brazil when I thought I'd lay it out there and try getting to know her.

She was sitting on the floor studying Spanish like she was cramming for a final exam. I thought I'd use this situation to introduce myself. And I was arrogantly confident that I could help her with her Spanish. I was an expert, after all, what with my two years of college-level Spanish. Ha, ha.

Her name was...is Julie. (I suppose you know that by the time you read this.) We quickly developed strong feelings for each other, enhanced by the unique situation we found ourselves in. To be sure, there were a couple of bumps along the way, not the least of which was when she called me the brother she never had. I cringed at that description, because when a girl says that to you, it typically ends all chance at romance.

But we were quickly falling in love, even though neither of us— having just signed up for two years of volunteer work—had in the slightest way expected or planned for love. Add to that the fact that after three months of training together in the capital city, we would go our separate ways to different villages across the little country of Paraguay.

In the end, though, love had its way. After only three months I asked your mother to marry me, and thankfully she said yes. After training we learned that our respective towns—mine Quiindy and hers Piribebuy—were about two hours apart via a rickety school bus ride. Since going our separate ways to these towns last August, we've still managed to spend many weekends together—alternating trips to the other's town—and getting to know each other and sharing our experiences.

We've spent many long nights talking about everything imaginable, sharing great books and even our letters from home. She especially loves when I read short stories to her by candlelight. We practice our Spanish together and we try to fit into the culture here as best we can. We experiment with the local cuisine—the mate, tereré, empanadas, and sopa paraguaya—and even the local practices of gardening and daily chores.

We try to fit into the culture, but at the same time we kinda live like a typical American couple, Julie heading off to her job at the local school, and me going to work at the credit union. It was both the worst of times—living via outhouse, outdoor shower, propane camping stove, and a cooler for a fridge—and the best of times. Sharing my life with someone, truly getting to know another person, was more impactful than I could have ever imagined.

We married last month courtesy of the local justice of the peace in Julie's little town of Piribebuy (pronounced Pee-dee-bay-bwee). We scrounged up enough money to travel by bus to the beaches of Brazil for a nice little honeymoon.

I've put off writing this current letter long enough. I guess your mom got all my attention since the minute I arrived in Paraguay. I knew that I better write this long overdue letter to you now, because it doesn't get any bigger than getting married!

It has been the strangest but most wonderful experience, living in this bizarre land and surviving on the utter basics while serving others. Meeting and having someone to share it with has made it even more worthwhile. The fact that our lives lack all the usual comforts has, in a strange way, been very rewarding.

Even something as basic as trying to get news from home and from around the world has been a challenge. But when we do get the news, albeit about a month late, it is very enjoyable to read. The Peace Corps generously buys subscription copies of the *U.S. News & World Report* magazine for all of us volunteers. Having no TV or radio, we became absorbed with some of the magazine's stories of things going on back home. Most notably, for us anyway, have been the stories of the Branch Davidians saga and a little-known story about a guy named Christopher McCandless.

Those two stories in particular gave Julie and me a lot to discuss in our abundance of free time. Those stories have gotten us debating the purpose of life, and where and how our relationship to God fits into that purpose. Julie, being a pretty devout Christian, converted me from being an unengaged Catholic to what I would call a newborn or *baby Christian*. She's got me really thinking hard about my faith, or my lack of it, up to this point in my life.

The Branch Davidians story, about a religious cult-like group, got me thinking about what my relationship with God is supposed to look like. It also got me thinking about how I as a Christian should be interacting with others.

The Chris McCandless story involves a guy about my age, who abandoned his own silver spoon life, kinda like I did. However, he also abandoned his family (cut all ties with them) in order to strike out to discover his own meaning of life. Chris' life ended tragically as he seemingly got in over his head trying to seek his purpose in far northern Alaska. He stupidly (in my opinion) headed into the Alaskan wilderness alone, and my guess is that he was about as skilled in wilderness survival as this suburban boy is.

Ultimately, they think Chris died of starvation after eating poisonous plants or something, and he was not able to make it back to civilization. He died on an abandoned school bus in the middle of nowhere, all alone in this world. A group of hunters found his body and his detailed diary, which is how we were able to read about it in the magazine.

Both this guy Chris and I were doing the same thing, in a way. That is, seeking the meaning of life and our purpose in it. How many other young people strike out to do the same, I wonder. Chris and I had the same goal, but we went about it in very different ways. I've done it in a more structured way, luckily—via the military, college, and now the Peace Corps—whereas Chris headed out West and eventually to Alaska, without any structure at all: no money, no connections, nothing. Maybe his story strikes me so deeply because I shudder when I realize that I could easily have taken his same path.

I also wonder what, if any, Chris' relationship was like with God. That thought hits me hard because I am only now waking up to God myself. Julie has truly sparked my interest, for the first time ever, in learning more about the faith that I have claimed to have all my life. I guess I was just going through the motions, even when growing up in Catholic grade school and high school. Now that I think about it, I doubt that I've even mentioned my relationship with God in any of my previous letters to you. Julie even has me reading the Bible daily. In fact, I am currently in the middle of reading it cover to cover for the first time. I am learning so much more than I ever knew about that good book.

It took me to go all the way to the middle of nowhere in South America to find God. Think about that! Kinda sad, but I guess God waits for us anytime and anywhere. While sad, I am obviously thankful that it finally happened. I'm honestly ashamed that I even called myself a Christian before, considering how little I knew about it all.

Well kids, I'll sign off for tonight, but I'm excited about what my future letters will contain, now that I have my partner to help make better sense of this thing called life.

Love,
Dad

P.S. – The contents of this letter come as a shock even to me. I never expected to meet my wife while here in South America. I think God is probably having a little laugh about it, making me come all the way to Paraguay to wake up and notice him for the first time, and with the help of my new wife who I met here.

I can't say that meeting your mom has completed my mission of discovering the answers to life, and my purpose in it, but it sure has shed some light on the issue. I now realize, embarrassingly, that I must look outside myself if I'm going to find those answers. I guess I was never going to have any hope of finding the answers while stuck in my own little universe.

Maybe that's another God joke: You can't find yourself if you're only focused on yourself.

At any rate, thanks to finding Julie I do fully realize that there are other perspectives about life besides my own. Duh! And having a strong-willed partner like your mom certainly makes that clear. It is a beautiful thing to realize...finally.

I feel renewed now that I have a partner to continue my journey with. Finding your partner in life alone cannot be life's answer, though. As you kids get older, don't fall for that false hope, that finding your soul mate is the end all, be all. That type of thinking could bring you more problems than solutions.

However, finding your life partner gives you a great advantage to finding life's answers and your purpose in this world.

One more funny thing to tell you: Your mom thinks it's weird that I'm writing these letters to people who haven't even been born yet. But I believe that, in some ways, she thinks it's cool that I'm writing letters to the kids I will have with her.

> *Therefore a man shall leave his father and mother and hold*
> *fast to his wife, and the two shall become one flesh.*
>
> *Ephesians 5:31*

TORRES DEL PAINE
Satisfying my Soul

But ask the beasts, and they will teach you; the birds of the heavens, and they will tell you; or the bushes of the earth, and they will teach you; and the fish of the sea will declare to you. Who among all these does not know that the hand of the Lord has done this?

Job 12:7-9

January 1994

Kids,

During our time here in the Peace Corps, your mother and I are trying to experience as much of the culture and sights that we can. On the meager wages that we get paid, it's a little hard to travel very extensively or do much of anything that costs a lot of money. But thankfully, things here are relatively cheap. It is inexpensive to live here, but for that very reason the Peace Corps pays us a stipend that is just enough to live like the locals.

As I mentioned in my last letter, we were able to afford a honeymoon week on the beaches of Brazil in the beautiful island city of Florianópolis (which means City of Flowers in Portuguese). That was back in April. We decided to save up for one more big trip while here in South America. We wanted to go to Machu Picchu in Peru, but it was too expensive. However, I honestly can say that the trip we decided to take—the one we are on a bus returning from right now—may have been equally as impressive.

We are returning from a whirlwind trip to the bottom of South America, which included extremely cool places like Santiago, Puerto Montt, the Strait of Magellan, and our ultimate destination, the Chilean national park called Torres del Paine. It's been a super long trip.

We first traveled by bus from Piribebuy to Santiago, the capital of Chile, and spent a couple of days exploring the city. Then we continued south on a 24-hour classic train ride to Puerto Montt, where we spent another day. I ate an eel sandwich (congrio) at a local diner there without realizing what I was eating. That was kinda funny. After a day in that quaint little seaside town, we hopped on another bus that took us all the way to Punta Arenas, and then another to Torres del Paine park. In all, we figure it's around 3,500 miles (one way) and we had to cross the Andes Mountains twice.

I can't even begin to describe the beauty of Torres del Paine, and the beauty is not merely in what the eyes can see. I really felt like I was in, well, God's personal park, because it was so absolutely quiet and peaceful there. There was only a smattering of other hikers—in fact, I'll bet we saw more alpacas than people during our days in the park. I guess it is so remote that it's not a popular park to travel to. Plus, I'm used to the state and national parks in the U.S., which are chock full of tourists compared to Torres del Paine.

Your mom and I were virtually alone in the park, hiking and camping for several days. It seemed like all we heard was each other and the wind. That made the experience just as breathtaking as the sights. The strange mountains, the glaciers, the numerous little flowers and plants, and the most aqua blue waters you ever saw in the various lakes around the park. Simply unbelievable!

And Torres del Paine wasn't the only awe-inspiring part of the trip. Spending New Year's Eve in the small town of Punta Arenas before heading into the park was surreal. I guess due to the holiday, most of the businesses were closed and the town was noticeably quiet. It was extremely bizarre, and this may sound silly, but I could truly feel that I was at the bottom of the world. Walking along the docks on the Strait of Magellan, hearing nothing but wind, seagulls, and the water hitting the shore had a sacred feel to it.

I could truly feel God's presence in that part of the world. It was humbling to experience the stark beauty of the snow-capped mountains at Torres del Paine, and the wonder of staring out over the Strait of Magellan to the *Land of Fire* and Antarctica beyond. I felt God looking down on us, pleased that we were able to experience one of his little-known parts of the world.

It was during those quiet days with your mom, in one of the remotest parts of the world, that another great realization hit me. I realized one new piece to the meaning of life, which is that God wants us to experience his creation to the fullest. I believe he wants to share all parts of his world with his people. God wants us to see, experience, and enjoy all the beauty that he created. I really believe this. I'm learning that God wants a lot from me, but I also think he wants me to stop and enjoy his beautiful creations.

Other places we've been able to experience in South America are Iguazu Falls and a few of the Jesuit missionary ruins in and around Paraguay. Both are utterly spectacular. Iguazu Falls makes our Niagara Falls look like a dripping faucet. If you watch a movie called *The Mission* with Robert De Niro and Liam Neeson, you can get a great feel for what these Jesuit missions are all about. Parts of Iguazu Falls are even shown prominently in the movie, but nothing compares to seeing that place in person. If you ever get a chance to come down here, you should, as those are two of the most breathtaking sights either of us have ever seen. Just like in Southern Chile, I truly felt the presence of God in these places.

Now, children, I would be failing you as your future dad if I didn't share a whole different reality that I have learned while here in South America. Yes, this continent has many stunningly beautiful places, a rich culture, and humble people who are the most kind and gentle folks you would ever meet. But as your mom and I have travelled around this continent, we've learned about some disturbing things since coming here.

There is an ugly side to this continent; yes, a number of truly dark histories have taken place in this land, just like in Europe. Beginning with the way the Spanish and Portuguese conquered the continent, which was bad enough. But these poor people have been ruled by some very horrible people over the decades since. Most recently have been numerous dictators terrorizing some of the countries here.

In fact, in all four of the countries I've visited—Paraguay, Brazil, Argentina, and Chile—the people were ruled with iron fists for many, many years, several until only a few years ago. Imagine that, dictatorships in South America as late as the 1980s. I've read stories of thousands of South Americans tortured, killed, or who simply *disappeared*. And there were more dictators than in just these four countries.

Making matters worse, I've read that our own country, the United States, had a hand in helping some of these dictators gain power, all in the name of preventing socialism from taking hold in our Western Hemisphere. I suppose our government decided that dictators—who brutalize their own people—were a safer bet than the threat of communism setting up shop in the region. Ugh.

And while not as impactful to the suffering peoples of South America, I learned about another ugly reality that happened throughout the continent. A number (possibly a very large number) of former German Nazis—yes, the World War II Nazis—escaped facing justice for their war crimes by fleeing to sites all over South America.

Imagine hundreds if not thousands of former Nazis hiding all throughout South America. Very unsettling. Your mom and I have seen a bunch of German influences down here as we pass through different towns and cities. It seemed odd at first, but not after I read about the post-WW2 influx of Germans. I read that in many cases these war criminals were hidden with the aid of their host countries' leaders.

As beautiful as the world can be, kids, you need to always realize that evil lurks just below the surface, if not higher. I share these unsettling realities about South America (and there are many more) because I want you to move through life with eyes wide open. I already told you about some of the ugly things that happened throughout Europe; and I barely touched the tip of the iceberg of that continent's horrifying history.

Just as there is beauty and wonder around the world, there is also ugliness and evil in all the same places. And what makes things even worse, in my mind, is that I'm starting to learn that a good degree of that ugliness is owned by the United States. I guess I was naïve growing up in the '80s, and being stationed in Europe, where it felt like we were purely and always the good guys. It reminds me of a Bible verse I read recently, something about "no one is blameless" or "none are innocent" or something like that. Nope, not even the good ol' U.S.A.

Well kids, we must always be mindful and awake about the fact that evil exists in this world. But we should not let it stop us from enjoying the beautiful things, places, and people that God has given us.

I look forward to writing you down the road.

Love,
Dad

P.S. – I'll end by reiterating that I was able to discover another piece of my *meaning of life* puzzle—that God wants us to enjoy his beautiful creations. He gave them to us for that very reason. After all, God gave Adam and Eve the Garden of Eden to enjoy.

But then I guess they screwed that up.

Wow, how ironic. Adam and Eve screwed up God's first beautiful garden, and the rest of us seem hell-bent on screwing up the rest of his creation. We insist on spoiling God's creation with so much evil and selfishness, just like Adam and Eve. I suppose that's not ironic at all, actually, unfortunately.

We humans are pathetic.

I'm starting to realize that things would be a whole lot better if more of us put God's wishes front and center, rather than our own. I'll try to formulate my thoughts on that for you in a future letter.

As it is written: None is righteous, no, not one.

Romans 3:10

EL PASO
Growing my Tribe

And he said to them, "Take care, and be on your guard against all covetousness, for one's life does not consist in the abundance of his possessions."

Luke 12:15

December 1995

Children,

Your mom and I returned to the U.S. last year and it truly feels like a different country after having lived in Paraguay. I don't know what happened in barely over two years, but things in the U.S. have changed a lot. Obviously, after living in a third world country for two years, everything is bound to appear bigger, better, and more beautiful than we ever remembered. But it's more than that.

There are all of a sudden a bunch of new places to shop, eat, and drink. We initially arrived back in the U.S. and spent a couple of months in little La Crosse, Wisconsin, visiting mom's family and friends. After that we went to Kentucky so that your mom could meet all my friends and family. In both places and everywhere in between, it looks like the country has exploded with new retail stores, restaurants, coffee shops, bars, and even lots of new food choices at the grocery stores.

Take just two examples: coffee creamer and ice cream. As far as I can recall, pre-Paraguay all we had were regular and nonfat dairy creamer, two types. Suddenly there are like ten different flavors of creamer. We thought we'd died and gone to heaven. And with ice cream, which I occasionally like, there are surprisingly lots of new brands and flavors to choose from, even what they call *premium* ice cream. Anyway, those are only two examples. The options for snacks, sugary drinks, frozen foods, and everything else appear endless.

And if that weren't enough, there are many restaurants and coffee shops around that I never saw before: Applebee's, O'Charley's, Chili's, and the Outback Steakhouse, complete with two-hour wait times to get in. That's just to name a few. Before I left for the Peace Corps, it felt like all we had were the fast-food joints (McDonald's, Arby's, Burger King, etc.), Bonanza and Ponderosa for a nicer dinner, and then the downtown restaurants that you take a date to. Today the choices seem to be unending. There are even tons of new breakfast/brunch places everywhere: Starbucks, Panera Bread, Atlanta Bread Company, and others.

Don't get me started on the retail shopping. A phenomenon called *big box stores* has emerged, and I honestly still can't believe it all, even after a year of being back. We have these huge hardware stores, for example, like Lowes and Home Depot. Pre-Paraguay all I remember was the local hardware stores or maybe a slightly larger Ace Hardware or Do It Best hardware. Now we have Lowes and Home Depot, which feel as big as an entire mall.

And there are similarly large specialty stores like Barnes & Noble bookstore, Media Play, Circuit City, and Best Buy, to name a few. You could spend half a day simply browsing stores like that. These big box stores are mostly specialty stores, such as Pier 1 Imports (home furnishings), AutoZone (car parts), Toys "R" Us (kids' toys and clothes), and Michaels (arts and crafts). The list goes on and on, and each of these specialty stores is humongous. It really blows my mind.

I can't help but compare these stores in the U.S.—with our plethora of product choices—with those in Paraguay. Mom and I, when we trekked into the capital city of Asunción to get our monthly paycheck, used to stop at the big supermercado (supermarket) that was popular mostly among Americans (of course). We thought we were in heaven because we could get nicer-than-usual foods from the wide selection of items (a greater selection than we had in our small villages, anyway). In our villages, we were lucky if the grocery stores were larger than an American convenience store like 7-Eleven. That is not an exaggeration.

Anyway, we thought that the grocery store in the capital of Asunción was big and great. Little did we know that only a few months later we'd return to an America where the Barnes & Noble bookstore was larger! I have mixed feelings about this. On one hand, I feel glad and proud to be an American, to be able to experience the ridiculous abundance that we have. But on the other hand, I often feel disgusted at the overabundance of what we have when compared to other people around the world. And the saddest part is that Americans don't have the slightest clue how abundantly they are living.

After having lived for two years with next to nothing in Paraguay, and now having more options than I can consume in a lifetime, it somehow makes me sad.

This place (our America) seems to have suddenly gone nuts with the amount of consumer options available to us. Don't get me wrong, it is very exciting for your mom and me. It feels like we live in Disney World every day. It's very strange, as if all of this snuck into America while we were gone. Maybe it had started before I left, while I was heads-down in college. Who knows. I only know that it doesn't resemble the America I grew up in. It's cool to have all these choices—as that is certainly American capitalism at its best—but the country feels more commercial because of it all, if that makes sense.

It doesn't feel as innocent anymore; everything feels plastic in some way. It's hard to put into words. *Artificial*, I believe that's the word I'm looking for. Everyone seems to be focused on all this stuff instead of on seeking deeper meaning in life. Maybe that's why it bothers me, because it feels like everyone but me is completely satisfied with this materialistic way of living.

It could be that I'm becoming an old fuddy-duddy already at age 29. Or perhaps it's because I'm a married adult. I don't know for sure, but I'm getting the feeling that the innocence of America is starting to disappear.

I just re-read the first part of this letter. Boy, that sounds kinda somber. I actually wanted to share some unbelievably great news, and that is that you, my little man Aleksandr, were born only a handful of days ago. So, these letters now have a physical audience of at least one!

I can't put into words my feelings. It's the strangest thing to be holding a little *me* in my arms. Let me back up a bit and give this event a bit of context.

We're presently living down here in El Paso, Texas. Upon exiting the Peace Corps, and after much thought, I decided to take a teaching job through a returned Peace Corps volunteer program. The program allows former volunteers to get paid a regular teacher's salary while still earning a teacher certification. The catch is that you must be willing to teach in one of the neediest (*undesirable* is a better word) areas of America, like inner cities, or on Native American reservations, or in my case, a stone's throw from the Mexico border. In other words, parts of the country where the demand for teachers is much higher than the supply.

So that's how we ended up in El Paso. We like it well enough here. It's as much like Paraguay as it is like the United States. Mom and I are definitely in the minority here, with more Spanish speakers than English speakers. The landscape (desert and mountains) is quite different than anything I've ever seen before, so it has been a cool experience in that sense. It is also pretty hot all year 'round.

Anyway, your birth this month of December felt like a little miracle for us. You see, it rarely ever snows in El Paso. But on the night you were born, son, literally while we were in the hospital bringing you into this world, it started snowing. You sure have given us the best Christmas we can imagine.

So, I am sitting here at the tail end of my Christmas break, and I knew I had to write a letter, seeing as how I now have a live audience. I'm not sure how many siblings you'll end up having, or how many grandchildren you'll give us, but these letters now go to at least you, little man.

I've been contemplating how your birth fits in with this big world, and my place in it, and what it means that you were blessed to have been born in this bountiful country of ours. More importantly, I'm trying to figure out what God's plan is for us. I'm finally starting to realize that my search for truth must involve God somehow. Your mother taught me that.

Over the Christmas break I've been considering my job as well. I don't think I was cut out to be a schoolteacher. I simply don't have the patience for these middle school brats. Especially because you are here, I want to focus on raising and teaching you in my spare time, and not be spending nights correcting papers for ungrateful kids and their parents. I'm sorry if I sound a little jaded, but things just aren't going well in my job, and I don't think teaching is the career for me.

And what that means is that mom and I are seriously talking about going back east after this first school year is completed. We'll probably take you back to meet everyone in Northern Kentucky and try for a fresh start. I'm confident we'll have more career opportunities if we move there. Kinda disappointing that we moved all the way out here for seemingly nothing.

I try not to look at things negatively like that, though. I'm glad we came out here to experience this strangely beautiful part of the United States. It certainly is unique and full of wonder, with the desert mountains, the variety of cactus-type plants, and interesting places like White Sands, Carlsbad Caverns, and neat mountain towns like Ruidoso and Cloudcroft. We'll always have these memories, and our memories of you being born here. I hope I can bring you back here someday to show you where it all started for you.

Until next time little bubba! I can't wait to experience every day with you.

Love,
Dad

P.S. – I now have many important things to think about, like what kind of job and career I'm going to get into so that I can provide a good life for you, your mom, and any other kids that come along. There are so many amazing things you can have in this country, that I want to give you kids whatever you want.

But as soon as I say that I feel ashamed for having said it. I need to check myself. It is going to be a challenge for me, and you, to focus on more meaningful things in life than just having *things*. I hope by the time you grow up, I will have a bunch of good answers and advice for you about how to navigate this complicated world.

Anyway, as you will learn by reading all my letters, my life's been pretty exciting thus far, but now I have your mom and you to take care of. Therefore, I need to settle down and get serious, as it were.

What to do, what to do?

All the ways of a man are pure in his own eyes, but the Lord weighs the spirit. Commit your work to the Lord, and your plans will be established.

Proverbs 16:2-3

COFFEY STREET
Building my World

*Many are the plans in the mind of a man, but it
is the purpose of the Lord that will stand.*

Proverbs 19:21

October 1999

My beautiful little children,

Yes, there are two of you now, as we brought a sister into the world
for you Alek. Autumn was born earlier this month and you are
loving every minute of being a big brother. She's just as cute as
you were as an infant. She looks at you with such amazing stares.
Something wondrous about infants—even at mere weeks old—is
that they clearly recognize their own, other little kids. She looks at
you with as much love as she looks at us, but I think more.

Autumn, we are so thrilled to add you to the family. You're a
beautiful little thing, and we can't wait to share the beauty of this
world with you. There is a lot to love in this world, but also a lot of

things to avoid. I will do everything I can to protect you from the evils of this world, but even more so, to show you all the beauty and wonder that it offers. After all, this is God's creation.

As I say that I realize how lucky I am to have this little family of mine, just as it is. I thank God for giving your mom to me because she re-introduced me to the Lord. I had always planned to raise my kids to know God, but I had lost my way until I met your mother. If I had met anyone else, there is a good chance that I would not be looking forward to raising you as Christians.

At the risk of contradicting myself, I must add that as excited as I am to be raising you kids as Christians, I am equally fearful. I am fearful because in the five years since mom and I returned from South America, this world—or should I say, this country—has been moving full speed toward a place that I no longer recognize. I can't clearly see where the world is headed, only that it is not pointed toward God, that's for sure.

The best way I can describe it is that the world seems to be bounding away from innocence as fast as it possibly can. By that I mean we are fleeing from everything that the Bible, and the United States that I grew up in, represent. You may be asking, "What exactly do the Bible and the country you grew up in have in common, Dad?"

Well, in my thinking, the United States of the 1970s and 1980s was a much better reflection of biblical teachings, at least for the common person. The country was a lot more innocent, a lot more family-oriented, and a lot more people were active, sincere Christians. We are very far from that place today.

Perhaps this is how life appears to all adults, when you have a family that you are responsible for. Maybe the world simply appears more selfish and cut-throat when you're a grown-up. I think there's more to it than that, however.

In the past five years, as if building my own world wasn't enough to stress me out, throw in the retail and consumer temptations that I mentioned in my last letter, and it feels like everything is moving too fast and out of our control. And by *our* I am referring to all Americans, and especially Christians.

It feels like in the blink of an eye, our country went from a place of honesty and innocence to an unrecognizable place full of fakes and frauds, decadence and depravity. America today feels like an elusive place of relativism and futility.

I guess I would say that America is becoming increasingly overwhelmed, stressed out, materialistic, and, well, the word *phony* comes to mind. And sadly, even though I write this being fully aware of what's happening around me, it is a daily battle to spare myself from what everyone else is falling into.

While I struggle to avoid all these negative things, I feel like a living, breathing oxymoron. On the one hand, I have this beautiful little wholesome family that follows the Lord and tries to stay close to what the Bible teaches, but on the other hand, I feel like I am slipping closer and closer toward the evils of this world. My conscious side wants to keep close to God's teachings, but my subconscious side wants to live entirely for the things of this world. Or maybe it's the other way around. I can't even tell anymore.

I'm starting to believe that getting married, having kids, and trying to start a career fills up your life and your mind so much that it's hard to keep it all together. Add to that trying to keep myself and my family on the straight and narrow path toward God. It feels like just as I add wonderful things to my life, I inadvertently add just as many burdensome things. I add a beautiful wife and kids to my life, but I also add stress and bills and debt. It's awfully frustrating.

I often wonder what it might have been like to stay in Paraguay and raise a family there, where we would be in the simplest of environments. Part of me wishes I could build an invisible Paraguayan border around my little world, kids and all, and live our own simple lives amid the chaos.

The world appears to be barreling toward overabundance and recklessness in all areas of life. This includes not only sinful things, but a general desire to have more and more of everything without any regard for the endgame. Let me give you a few examples.

I haven't even touched on computers and the internet yet. And I have a sense that this has something to do with why everything appears to be moving so fast. We had computers in the late '80s, but they were really nothing more than glorified electric typewriters that could send your documents to a printer. But as soon as we returned from Paraguay and started our lives in El Paso, we soon got our own home computer.

Having your own computer and getting on the internet can be great. I can keep in touch with people by email, I can look up information on any topic imaginable, and I can apply for jobs through the internet (no more mailing resumes on watermarked paper, thank goodness). It is an amazing thing to have, and yet it is so vast and unbelievable. It's like we've darted light years ahead of ourselves in just a few years.

So that's the situation with the internet and computers. I'm sure I'll have more to say about it in future letters, because it seems like they come up with new ways to make life easier every day. But like I said, I have this sense that the internet is a big reason why it feels like we are barreling toward no good.

Other things that make me feel sad for our lost innocence are in the movies, TV shows, and music. I'm sure I sound like an old grandpa saying this, but my goodness, it is getting increasingly dirty (or evil) every year. These people seem to make a specific point of referring to sex, drugs, lying, cheating, and stealing from others, and it's in every song, movie, TV show, and even in TV commercials. That's what I mean when I say that the country that I grew up in was much more in line biblically than it is today. Not that I was ever so innocent in my youth, but it is way more out in the open these days, and always pushing the limits.

Anyway, all of this is my lengthy explanation for why I am fearful about trying to raise you kids as Christians in the world today. I'm beginning to realize that this is not going to be as easy as I thought it would be. It would have been much easier if I could have raised you in the same world I grew up in.

It is a constant battle trying to resist the temptations to live like everybody else, and slip into consumerism and materialism and all the trappings of this world. I've fallen into it already without even realizing it, into the mindset that we have to have all the material comforts. Yes, our modest little house here on Coffey Street is filled with all the modern conveniences. While we live pretty humbly compared to many others, we have much more than we need, deserve, or can afford (our credit card balance is proof of that). I have mixed feelings about all of this trying to keep up with the Joneses.

We purchased a lot of things in El Paso, and even more since moving back to Cincinnati, as we got caught up in the hype of wanting to have all the stuff that other people have. It's really sad, now that I think about it, that mom and I went from having close to nothing in Paraguay, to being in pretty serious debt, in a matter of just over a year.

On the bright side, I guess, I have started to settle into a career that I enjoy, that can hopefully pay for all this stuff that we keep buying. I've started doing writing and editing work, first for a textbook publisher, and now writing and editing for a small-town newspaper and for a few internet news websites. I guess it's safe to say that computers and the internet are here to stay. I'm starting to see how they can actually help me in my career.

Anyway, while I like this new career, I can say with conviction that I will never look to my career as the meaning of life. Work is what we all must do. The Bible even talks about that. But I feel like in today's world, if we aren't careful, our work becomes a means to pay for all the stuff we want. Our work should have more meaning than that. Nowhere in the Bible does it say we should work hard so that we can have more stuff. Unfortunately, too many of us, myself included, do go to work simply to maintain a certain lifestyle. I fear I am falling into that trap.

And while I'm falling, I'm trying to keep my head above the herd to continue my search for my ultimate purpose and for truth. It is hard though, continuing my search while at the same time slipping into the trap of materialism and living the so-called *American Dream*.

Love,
Dad

P.S. – Kids, it sincerely is the greatest conundrum to try to resist the temptation in America to have it all. Once you start creating a family, the desire to give your family everything is irresistible. You'll convince yourself that you should buy everything and go into extreme debt so that you can give your family (and yourself, who am I kidding) everything you think they need or deserve.

This is the reality I am in right now, kids. I truly hope I can figure out this mystery called life in time to share the answer with you. At least before you grow up and repeat my mistakes like this mistake of falling into consumerism. As great as it is to have all the cool things that this world offers, I know deep down that that is not the meaning of life, to have it all. There is no truth in it.

But those who desire to be rich fall into temptation,
into a snare, into many senseless and harmful desires
that plunge people into ruin and destruction.

1 Timothy 6:9

CALVARY ROAD
Drowning in this World

And whatever my eyes desired I did not keep from them. I
kept my heart from no pleasure, for my heart found pleasure
in all my toil, and this was my reward for all my toil. Then
I considered all that my hands had done and the toil I had
expended in doing it, and behold, all was vanity and a striving
after wind, and there was nothing to be gained under the sun.

Ecclesiastes 2:10-11

May 2013

Kids,

Where, how, did I get so far off track?

I look back and see that it's been more than 13 years since the last
letter I've written to you. And as I contemplate all that's happened
since that last letter—since Autumn joined us and our little family
became complete—it is not difficult to see how I went astray. The
priorities that I placed front and center sent me down the wrong

path and caused a ripple effect that hurt and neglected the ones I love the most.

Not only did I go astray from living as a Christ follower, which is what I've claimed to be trying to do ever since starting a family, but I also went grossly astray from anything remotely resembling a virtuous purpose for my life.

I have fallen victim…no, that's not the right word…I have fallen guilty, yes guilty, of following down the path of living for this world. My life has become a quest for more money so I can buy more stuff for my family and myself, and I threw everything else aside. And I lied to myself the whole time I was doing it. The irony of all ironies is that much of the stuff I acquired was entirely unnecessary, unless you count trying to keep up with the Joneses as being necessary. Sadly, many Americans around me also fall into this trap.

But succumbing to materialism is not the only thing I've been guilty of. Since my last letter, a new phenomenon has taken over this world that has consumed people's lives just as much as materialism. It raises the sin of *keeping up with the Joneses* to an unachievable level. That phenomenon is something called social media. Let me explain, even though by the time you read this, you'll know full well what it is. And I shudder to think what social media will be like as you grow up in this world. So please heed my warnings about this.

I can't even remember when the term social media came about, or when the popular websites came to be in common usage by the common person. I guess it started with a website called Myspace, where you sign up as a member and then you can connect with people all over the world through Myspace. This includes family and relatives, old friends from high school, and even perfect strangers, for that matter. Myspace was soon replaced by Facebook, and then came Twitter, and most recently Instagram, as well as various others.

All these sites basically do the same thing, which is to help you share as much of your personal life and your opinions as you care to, with your personal group of friends and family, or with the rest of the world. And trust me, it doesn't take long for you to believe that the entire world cares what you have to say and share. That's one of the primary dangers and sins of social media, I'm now convinced.

Social media boosts your ego way beyond where it should be, your pride greater than it should be. And without realizing it, you're soon comparing all parts of your life against everyone else's. Meanwhile, it tosses humility, kindness, responsibility, and authenticity out the window.

It all seemed so great at first, being able to connect instantly to people you've lost touch with over the years, either due to time, our busy lives, or friends and loved ones moving away. The problem, though, is that it becomes addicting, and ultimately becomes a contest—either legitimate or fake (it's difficult to tell which)—to brag about your life and how great it is.

My main problem, and I'm sure this is a problem for millions of other people, is that I became more concerned with the people I'm connected to on social media than I was concerned with my own family and close friends. I started to neglect my family—you two and your mom—because I was more interested in keeping up with the Joneses of Facebook. I cared far more what people on Facebook thought about me than what my own wife and children thought about me. I've been more interested in impressing people I didn't even know than growing my relationships with my loved ones.

As I re-read my last letter to you, I cringed as I read it, because I more or less warned myself that I was headed down this very path. I had become so wrapped up in my own little universe, my own pleasures and problems, that I lost sight of everything of true importance. And perhaps saddest of all, I have become one of *those Christians*, the type that proclaims to be a devout believer, but who still lives like everyone else.

Pastors often challenge us with this question: "How does your life as a Christian look any different from the lives of non-Christ believers?" And this: "If you were in a courtroom, and a jury had to find you guilty of being a Christian, would there be enough evidence to convict you?"

My answers to those two questions have regrettably been "Not at all" and "No," respectively.

You may be wondering what woke me up from this pathetic state of my life? How did I become aware of my folly?

Two of my own family members—in your own unique ways—essentially told me that you hate me and want nothing to do with me. In a few more words than that, your mom told me that not only am I not her best friend, but that she absolutely doesn't care about me at all anymore. This was all a direct result of my selfish, and self-centered, living.

You, Alek, woke me up when you told your friend what my main problem is, in an indirect kind of way. And you said it right in front of me, as if I wasn't even there. You and your friend were working on your truck in the garage. I came out and scolded you about not making a mess of the garage, rather than offering to help or even showing interest in what you were doing. You turned to your friend and said, "See, all he ever does is want to correct me, rather than help."

How utterly humiliating, for me.

It took those two ugly encounters—which occurred back-to-back—to finally bring my failures to my attention. It breaks my heart that I was completely oblivious to how I have been behaving these past years. I am so deeply sorry to both of you and to your mom that I've behaved this way and have been a failure as a dad and as a husband.

I've been reflecting on all of this since it became apparent to me, and all I can say for the moment is that I'm deeply sorry to both of you for not being the kind of dad you surely wished I was. But I can also vow that I am going to make a number of serious changes moving forward. Honestly, I'm partly glad that this all came to light in the way that it did. I only wish it had come to light years ago.

Since being forced to face the reality of my relationships, it didn't take a ton of reflection to realize what I've got to work on from here on out. I need to make this stupid social media much less prominent in my life, if not remove it completely. And I've got to stop living like the rest of the idiotic, materialistic world and quit trying to keep up with the Joneses. There is nothing Godly or Christian about any of it.

Worse still, those things clouded my life from seeking my true purpose and ultimate truth.

It became so bad that I completely forgot about these letters that I've wanted to continue writing to you kids. It explains why 13 years have passed since my last letter. I forgot to write to you because I also forgot about, or abandoned, my search for truth and my purpose in life.

And this is all the result of me falling so horribly far off track this past decade plus. I've neglected both my family and my search for meaning in life. Worst of all is that I abandoned everything I've learned since meeting your mother about following Christ.

All I can say is that I make a promise to you that I will work harder to focus more on you, your mom, God, and my true self. I honestly hate having to state those words because I know that words alone mean nothing. We will simply have to see if I make good on that promise in my future actions.

Love,
Dad

P.S. – I've been pondering all the things I've written to you about my life, my misguided efforts at searching for truth and purpose in my life. I'm embarrassed now to read what I thought were the answers to life: fun, partying, adventure, and worldly wisdom. Many of my beliefs were shameful, immature, and depraved. I'm tempted to tear up all of my letters to this point and start over. I feel like my life has been an utter waste…I haven't learned anything it seems.

And as shameful as all those previous beliefs were, being misled by the trappings of this world *after* I was introduced to the Lord and *after* I claimed to be a good Christian, that this is far worse. This past decade has been the most shameful time of my entire life.

I pray daily that I can start forsaking the trappings of this world. I also pray that you kids learn from my mistakes. And I pray that you abandon the evils of this world, evils disguised as worthy pursuits and pleasures.

Do not be deceived: God is not mocked, for
whatever one sows, that will he also reap.

Galatians 6:7

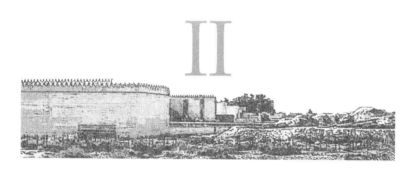

Waking Up from Babylon

Then Jesus told his disciples, "If anyone would come after me, let him deny himself and take up his cross and follow me. For whoever would save his life will lose it, but whoever loses his life for my sake will find it. For what will it profit a man if he gains the whole world and forfeits his soul? Or what shall a man give in return for his soul?"

Matthew 16:24-26

4TH & WALNUT
Finding Purpose

You felt secure in your wickedness, you said, "No one sees me";
your wisdom and your knowledge led you astray, and you
said in your heart, "I am, and there is no one besides me."

Isaiah 47:10

February 2014

Kids,

Since *waking up* last year, I'm beginning to see all things much more clearly. Specifically, I'm realizing the futility of living like everyone else in the world. It's going to take some time to break my bad habits, but I'm determined to do so and start living a different life. A life where I give time to the things that are important: God, family, and truth.

Recently, I realized something very noteworthy, which is that many millions of my fellow Americans are trapped living in never ending cycles. What I mean by this is that people's lives are on a seasonal cycle of pleasures and distractions, moving along a circular pattern that has no beginning, no end, and which leads to nowhere, to nothing.

The things people do, year in and year out, is a non-stop repeat cycle of preoccupations they spend their time and energy on...until they die. This includes everything from following sports teams to escaping with every popular new TV series, and even to getting excited about different seasonal holidays. For example, many people start the year by making New Year's resolutions, followed by hunkering down for the winter to watch basketball for a few months, then to attending spring, summer, and fall sporting events and festivals, which merges into celebrating the fall and winter holidays. And then they do it all over again. And then another year. And then another. And another.

Last year, for example, we collectively headed to the movie theaters to see more Avengers' movies, another Hunger Games movie, and another Hobbit movie. Next year we'll do the same for the next set of movies. And if we weren't headed to the movies, we were sitting at home watching *The Big Bang Theory*, *Dancing with the Stars*, or *The Voice*. And next year we'll watch them again, and possibly add even more shows to our routine. In sports, the Seahawks just won the Super Bowl, the Red Sox won last fall's World Series, and the Louisville Cardinals won the NCAA championship. Those are the sports I would follow, but of course everybody has their own favorites. This coming year will have all new champions, of course. And on and on it goes.

And so every year passes, every sports season ends and begins again, we celebrate each holiday only to look forward to the next, all the while heading down a path to nowhere.

I guess this is how people live, sadly, when they live for this world and this world only. That's how I spent those 13 years that I mentioned in my last letter to you, until I woke up. It makes sense that this is how you would live if you thought that this world is all there is—in a never-ending cycle of pleasures and distractions, buying and then discarding a never-ending pile of consumer goods.

And yet, I can't help but notice that all of this occurs while at the same time we go to and from our jobs, passing by each other without giving much thought to one other. We're all in our own little universe, worried only about ourselves and our own satisfactions. We not only pass by each other, but we also pass by those in need. We pass by those who don't have the luxury to dwell on sports teams and TV shows. Many people out there are truly suffering, and right in our own communities. They may be homeless. They may be suffering other forms of poverty, job loss, depression, or many other serious problems. But of course, we don't notice any of this because we're stuck in our cycle.

And this whole thing with the internet and social media, as I've mentioned, is only making matters worse. Social media serves only to focus our attention on ourselves and our status in comparison to others. So now more than ever, people are looking inward when they should be looking outward. The people who need people aren't getting any attention, because we're so focused on ourselves and our own problems and pleasures.

I think what has helped me wake up to this is a unique relationship I've had for the past few months. I'm talking about a new friend I have, a guy named Mike. You've never met Mike; in fact, no one else that I know is aware of Mike. Now that I mention it, I wonder just how many people are aware of Mike?

Anyway, Mike is a homeless guy who I've struck up a relationship with recently. In my current job in downtown Cincinnati, I walk to work each morning about six blocks from the parking lot. Mike is always there at the corner of 4th and Walnut, about a block from where I work.

Like many other homeless folks, Mike carries a coffee can in which he hopes to collect money. He doesn't hold a sign of any sort; he just holds the coffee can out and hopes for donations.

Early on when I first saw Mike, instead of giving him money I started bringing him a cup of coffee when I stop to get my own. And about once a week I also bring Mike a bagel with cream cheese. Every day that I see him we'll talk for about five minutes just to chat about whatever. Since we are both Cincinnati natives, we have plenty to talk about.

Sometimes Mike wants to talk about how he needs bus money to go here or there around town, sometimes to doctor appointments, or other times to visit family members or friends. I'll often give him a dollar or two if I have it on me.

Not being a medical professional, I can't pinpoint Mike's medical issues. However, it feels to me like he has some type of mental problems because he struggles with managing common tasks, tasks that most people take for granted. Making matters worse, Mike has to worry about his safety and well-being around other homeless people, especially in the homeless camp where he tries to sleep at night.

One week when I knew that the winter temperatures were going to get very, very cold, I bought him a pair of gloves, a sock hat, and a backpack because I noticed he never had these things. I knew these things would be useful to him. But the very next time I saw him he said that the items were stolen from him by someone in the camp.

I bring this up to tell you that there is a whole other reality of this country that nobody appears to want to acknowledge. I think most of us try our best to ignore it. I'm talking about the suffering of our fellow man.

I recently heard about a survey taken of homeless people. They were asked, "What is the hardest thing about being homeless?" I was shocked and saddened to learn that the most common response was that they feel invisible.

After having spent time with Mike, it occurred to me how incredibly sad a reality this must be. Mike is such a nice guy who seems to be in his predicament merely due to some medical issues and bad breaks in life. He is as interesting to talk to as anyone else in the city, and yet most days he probably also feels invisible. That is the kind of thing that will truly kill one's spirit, feeling invisible as people pass by you, trying desperately to avoid eye contact.

I'm happy that I struck up this relationship with Mike, but I also feel ashamed that it's taken all my life to understand these things. Anyway, my relationship with Mike has helped me to finally start to see what my purpose in life should be, and should have been all along. And that is to open my eyes and my heart to others instead of only looking out for myself. I've spent the past decade or so thinking only about myself. Sure, I donated a bit to different causes at church or through the mail, but I never opened up to others on a personal, face to face level.

I'm so ashamed and I feel so foolish, because I know that many of the verses in the Bible, particularly in the New Testament, teach us to love others as we love ourselves. And here I am just now realizing this. Despite my blind spots, I thank God for placing this truth front and center in my life, even if it did take longer than expected.

Love,
Dad

P.S. – How ironic is it that I look forward to talking to a homeless guy each day more than to anyone else? And that my conversations with him are much richer and more valuable than any conversations I have on social media? I guess I shouldn't be surprised. In fact, it makes perfect sense to me...now.

Would others who are addicted to social media agree? Would they even see Mike as they pass by with their faces in their phones?

Could there ever be an opening in the never-ending cycle of people's lives, an opening that would allow someone like Mike to slip in? Perhaps not, not without an awakening like the one I've recently had. (Thank you, God, for finally waking this fool up.)

If it does take a wakeup call, like the one I had, to change people's hearts and minds, then I pray that everyone gets that wakeup call.

"And a second is like it: You shall love your neighbor as yourself."

Matthew 22:39

PADUCAH
Acknowledging Him

And one of them, a lawyer, asked him a question to test him. "Teacher, which is the great commandment in the Law?" And he said to him, "You shall love the Lord your God with all your heart and with all your soul and with all your mind. This is the great and first commandment. And a second is like it: You shall love your neighbor as yourself."

Matthew 22:35-39

September 2016

Children,

It's been a couple of years since my last letter. I want to begin by continuing one of the points I made in my last letter about the emptiness of many Americans' lives.

I first want to share with you what's going on in the current culture, as I did in the last letter. At the movies, in an apparently never-ending cycle, we've had even more movies about superheroes,

Disney characters, Star Wars, and Hunger Games to entertain us. Even the old favorites like James Bond, Mission Impossible, and the Jurassic dinosaurs are reappearing. If I didn't know better, I'd swear that Hollywood is trying to make my point for me: that this world offers nothing but empty entertainment to fill our time as we trudge down a path to nowhere.

It reminds me of a verse out of Ecclesiastes: *What has been is what will be, and what has been done is what will be done, and there is nothing new under the sun. (Ecclesiastes 1:9)*

That book of the Bible is fast becoming one of my favorites, as it points out the futility of trying to live for this world. But I digress.

Just as in the movies, in sports it's all the same, too. The Broncos won the last Super Bowl, the Royals won the last World Series, and Villanova won the last NCAA men's basketball tournament. Every year a different team wins, or sometimes the same team wins. It doesn't matter. The more I think about sports in this country the more laughable it is to me. People obsess over their favorite sports' teams year after year after year after year, while their life whittles away. I'm sure they miss the irony that the sports seasons will continue after they die, and the players won't even notice each dead fan's absence. The advertisers might notice, but no one else.

And while I'm sure it only feels this way, but politics also seems to be captivating everyone's life nowadays. This is because two of the nastiest people you can imagine—Hillary Clinton and Donald Trump—are currently facing off for the presidential election in a couple of months. Truthfully, it's just one more thing that has overtaken the hearts and minds of people who can't see beyond this life. Even many Christians are consumed by all of this.

Over the past several years, I've spent many, many hours studying the Bible. A theme that comes up repeatedly is the theme of God's people becoming overly consumed with their day-to-day troubles and their worldly affairs. The Bible consistently talks about the logic for, and the need to, look to God and Jesus Christ instead of obsessing on our desires, our cares, and our problems in this life. The good book reminds us to place our worries in God's hands and to instead keep our focus on loving him, loving others, and on our life after this earthly life.

But do we do that? No.

The cares of this world weren't supposed to be the focus of this letter. But when I observe how everyone around me lives (which is how I used to live) I'm laughably disgusted by the utter pointlessness of many things that go on in our country. The utter waste of what we spend our money on, what we give our attention to, where we seek pleasures, and what we set as our goals in life. The most advanced nation on Earth, advancing toward emptiness!

As far as our little family goes, we've all made big changes recently. Alek you left for the Navy two years ago, and the rest of us moved down to Florida soon after. I think we are all hoping that our changes of scenery will help us in the search for how best to live our lives. I pray we realize that giving attention to God and our fellow man is more important than where we live or what careers we strive for.

What I wanted to tell you about in this letter is another individual I encountered recently, another person that I believe God sent my direction.

Let me give you a bit of background first. I've recently been working—and for all intents and purposes living—in Memphis, Tennessee working a contract job for Nike. Last weekend, instead of flying home, I decided to stay in the area and drive up to Paducah, Kentucky for their big annual BBQ festival. I rented a room at a B&B within walking distance of the festival site, right in the old downtown area.

Now, let me preface what I'm about to tell you with a warning that you must heed. If, or hopefully when, you decide to forsake this world to truly follow Christ, it's not going to be easy. The world, or Satan (am I being redundant?), will continuously try to pull you back into focusing on, if not worshipping, the things of this world. That has happened to me numerous times since my awakening a few years ago, and I expect to continue facing this challenge in the future. It certainly happened to me on this weekend road trip.

In the span of about ten hours, during my visit to the BBQ festival in Paducah, I received the revelation of another big piece of the puzzle of my life, my search for purpose and for truth.

After checking into the B&B, I walked down to the festival with the intent of enjoying the food and drink available, with hopes of meeting some new friends to party with, so to speak. *Party with the locals* at their big BBQ festival, that was my foolish plan.

Well, I did enjoy the food and drink, and I did chat with a few of the locals, but as the minutes and hours played out, it occurred to me that I didn't fit into that scene at all. To be completely honest, I was feeling disappointed about this, and embarrassed.

The only person that I struck up a halfway meaningful conversation with was a guy in a wheelchair who also was sitting alone in the beer gardens near me. We had a friendly conversation. He was a local and I was asking him about the area, the festival, etc.

During the conversation I realized that God was most certainly sending me a message. I think he was sending the same message that he sent me back on 4th and Walnut (with my homeless friend Mike), which is to seek out and love others. God was telling me to stop focusing on my own fun in this world and instead seek something higher. I was feeling out of place in that festive environment, and the only person who bothered to spend meaningful time with me was another loner like myself. Yes, that was clearly a message.

I received the message loud and clear, and decided I needed to end this charade of trying to fit in in this world...once again. So, after my friend and I parted ways, I headed back to the B&B to call it a night.

But a funny thing happened as I arrived back at the B&B about 10:00 p.m. The home's handyman/cook/manager, named Wade, was still awake as I opened the front door. Before leaving for the BBQ festival earlier in the day, we had merely exchanged pleasantries. I expected to just say good night and head up to my room. However, we began talking about random things, beginning with what I thought of the BBQ festival. I shared what I saw and did there, what foods I sampled, etc. I commented on how much I loved small towns like Paducah and longed to live in a similar place.

The more Wade and I talked the deeper our conversation got. We each shared our backgrounds, particularly on family and our relationship with Christ. Wade talked about his struggles of being a single dad, trying to make ends meet while giving his young son as normal an upbringing as possible.

I shared that, while I didn't have those daily struggles anymore (since my kids were older and our lives a little more established), I did share how I was also in Wade's shoes, so to speak, when we were getting our little family started. I shared that my greatest struggles lie in trying to keep focused on what truly matters in life, and the constant struggle to fight off the temptations of this world.

Our midnight chat led to a discussion about how people's lives veer from their intended purpose, the purpose God wants for them. Wade had some incredibly insightful things to share about our current world vs. Gods' dream for us as his children. He shared something I'd never heard before. He said that above all, God wants us to worship him constantly, not because he is selfish or jealous. Rather, since God knows that he is the perfect representation of truth, he wants us to experience that truth.

I became mesmerized with the things Wade was telling me. Here in this tiny corner of the world, on a random weekend, from the simplest young man you could imagine, came words of wisdom greater than you would find on any university campus or from the pulpit of any TV evangelist.

As I listened to Wade, at one point I honestly started wondering if I was speaking to Jesus Christ himself, in disguise. I have often heard the suggestion that Jesus disguises himself as a homeless person, in order to see how we might react to him. Interesting to think about. Wade could have even passed as Jesus in the images that we think of when we picture Christ. He sure had the persona of Christ, as he was so calm and loving in everything he shared.

Wade and I talked until about 3:00 in the morning, before we realized we both needed to hit the sack. But we continued our conversation a bit more later in the morning before I left town. What was so enticing...no, it was addicting...was the overriding message that Wade was sharing. And that message is that he is, and the rest of us should be, absolutely obsessed with loving Jesus Christ and his Father, our heavenly Father. Wow, so obvious yet so powerful!

Love,
Dad

P.S. – I hope you kids take to heart all my letters, but especially the last two. For a half century I've been wandering this Earth, and I am only now fully understanding the truth, and what my simple purpose in life should be. I've known of the two Great Commandments since I was a kid—to love God with all my heart, all my soul, and all my mind, and to love my neighbor as myself— but it took until adulthood to fully see and understand this truth.

Maybe I thought the answer to life had to be more complex than this directive from the Bible. Perhaps I was hoping for something more exciting or meaningful, by human standards. All my life I'd been listening to the various things that the world claims are the answers to life. But it turns out I was going to the wrong source— the world—for answers. The answers were right there in the book that I've had access to my whole life.

P.P.S. – Finally, I need to point out a revelation I've had from one of my earliest letters. As a kid, when I was getting ready to leave for the military, I wrote to you that I feared I was forgetting to take something with me on my adventure. And I told you that I wished I could take my dad and a best friend with me on that adventure.

I now realize that it was God and Jesus that I was forgetting. They were the dad and best friend I was forgetting.

Which causes me to wonder, "How different would my life have been if I had remembered to keep God and Jesus with me all those years?" Maybe I still would have gone to all the same places in life, but how different would it have been if God and Jesus were with me the whole time?

That they should seek God, and perhaps feel their way toward him and find him. Yet he is actually not far from each one of us.

Acts 17:27

MAJESTIC WAY
Uncovering the Truth

*The fear of the Lord is the beginning of wisdom, and
the knowledge of the Holy One is insight.*

Proverbs 9:10

July 2019

Kids,

I'm writing this from the little cottage we're staying at in Sequim, Washington. So many things have changed as you kids have gotten older. I can't believe we're out here in Washington visiting Alek as you wrap up your time in the Navy. The rest of us have been in Florida for five years already. All these changes have been good, however, because I can see that focusing on our relationships with God and family have led us to some good places.

It's kinda nice knowing that as the rest of the world plods along in its usual ways, each of us are plotting our own unique courses. I guess your mom and I have had a good influence on you two, as neither of you seem to have the need to compare yourselves to others. Autumn, you learned quickly just how nasty people can be on social media, and so you bowed out from that world early on, for the most part. I know it stinks to realize how evil people can be in how they treat others online, and how the comparisons and trying to out-do one another can be all-consuming. I am grateful that you learned these lessons early and thus avoided getting seriously hurt by people in the idiotic virtual world. I love seeing your dedication to working hard at your job and your schoolwork, and I love that you chose a very a practical major and career to pursue, rather than go for a trendy college and a socially *woke* major.

Alek, you also altogether avoided ever comparing yourself to others, both online and in the so-called real world. I still laugh at the way you announced to us that you were joining the Navy. You shocked us and your friends, as your decision came out of nowhere. You have been a leader and a trend-setter in your own right. You completely ignore and don't care about what other individuals, or society as a whole, are up to. You have your own dreams and goals, and you simply go for them. I love that. And God probably has a chuckle watching you ignore all of society every day, every year, as you do your own thing. God likes when we ignore the things of this world.

Sadly, the online world has taken over as the current cultural trend. All anyone seems to talk about or concern themselves with is their life on social media. People spend hours a day just scrolling through their different social media accounts: Facebook, Instagram, Twitter, and the newest fad, TikTok. People are far too focused on how many *likes* they get—how popular, cool, and interesting they can make themselves appear. It doesn't matter if their online persona is real or true, only how popular they appear. It doesn't even matter if they themselves know they are exaggerating their true life. All that matters is what other people think of them.

I think social media has accelerated the erosion of truth, our curiosity for truth, even the slightest interest in truth.

As much as I love to see that you kids have grown into independent-minded young adults, I hope you go the extra steps to be extremely anti-society by living for God, making that your number one priority in life. As all my earlier letters show, it took me too many years to figure this out.

Being independent-minded is a great characteristic to have, but worthless if you don't use it to seek out and embrace the truth. I hope you don't take as long as I did to realize that we should put all our focus on loving God and loving others, the lessons I mentioned in my last two letters.

I learned one more very emphatic lesson recently, which is why I need to write you today.

As you know, your grandpa passed away very recently. The lesson I received happened in my dad's final days. Grandpa's health quickly went downhill over the past year, and really worsened fast in his last six months. In his final few weeks, we had to keep putting him in the hospital on Pasadena Avenue, or in the nursing home on Majestic Way, and then back home again. Thankfully, everything was within a mile of home for dad because this happened several times—back and forth between the hospital, the nursing home, and home.

Just a few days before he died, I was visiting dad in the nursing home with my mom. Toward the end of the visit, I told dad that I would continue praying for him to get well soon. Dad said he wasn't sure if he was going to get well anymore. This comment almost made me cry, because I recalled my older brother recently telling me that dad couldn't believe this was actually happening to him already, at the age of just 84.

At this point words flowed from my mouth that I don't think I was controlling. I said something like, "Well dad, if you're not going to get well anymore, then that simply means you're going to be with Jesus soon. And that's the main point of this life anyway, right?"

Dad replied with something that surprised me. He said, "Kurt, I don't know if I'm going to make it in."

Somehow, I was able to keep myself from bawling at this point, and I said, "Dad are you kidding? You're one of God's princes. They can't wait for you to join them."

He chuckled and said, "Maybe you're right. I sure hope so."

I have no idea where my words came from. I've never called anyone a *prince* before. In fact, I've never even thought of the concept of God having princes. But as I left the nursing home that day, I thought about that exchange, and I realized that it's true. The Bible talks about how we will be given special roles in heaven, based on how we showed our faithfulness here on Earth. I don't claim to understand how it all works, but I know enough to know that my dad should not have been doubting his afterlife.

Don't worry kids, there is no doubt in my mind that your grandpa is living eternally with Jesus right now. He was most likely moved to the front of the line at the gates of heaven. In fact, he was probably given a special VIP pass so that he could mingle with the likes of Moses, Abraham, and the apostles.

Your grandpa was a Christian giant here on Earth, living as a perfect example of what a true Christian is. His life was an excellent example for us to follow.

However, that whole exchange got me thinking about those people who do lay on their deathbed terrified that they haven't been *good enough* to enter heaven. It makes my heart weep that many people have this incorrect understanding of eternity. This idea that we must earn our way into heaven is an incorrect understanding of salvation.

Millions of Christians fail to see that we don't need to *earn* our way into heaven, but rather that we simply need to (sincerely) accept Jesus Christ as our Lord and Savior and repent of our sins. The way we live our lives would then reflect whether we truly did accept Christ as our Savior and that we are living in a fashion to avoid sin.

How we live our life is the *proof* that we have indeed accepted Christ and repented of our sins. The proof would be that we are striving every day to live as God would want us to.

I was raised with those same flawed beliefs, and for the longest time I too thought that I had to earn my way into heaven; that my good deeds had to outweigh my sins. If that is your outlook on life, you would forever be living in a competition with yourself: good deeds vs. bad deeds. How stressful and unnerving that would be.

It saddens me to think that so many people have that mindset. And then, when they are on their deathbeds, they must no doubt wonder who they will join after they pass: Christ or Satan. How horrible to have those thoughts.

The truth, children, and this may be the ultimate truth of all truths, is that none of us can earn our way into heaven. We are too sinful. Yes, all of us. We cannot do it on our own. We need God's mercy to earn salvation. The good news is that he offers that to us.

We only need to acknowledge that God's son came to Earth and died for our sins, the sins that are enough to keep us out of heaven. Jesus took our sins upon himself. Again, we merely have to accept him as our Lord and Savior, repent for our sins, and then *live a life that reflects our belief that we are indeed saved.*

You can tell the people who truly accept Christ as their Savior and have sincerely repented for their sins. You can tell because their life looks vastly different from their former selves and from the rest of society. Their life reflects their Christian beliefs in every way.

Moreover, a true Christian wouldn't be the least bit worried or scared when they are on their deathbed. In fact, Christians should all look forward to that glorious day when we die on this Earth. Because that is when the truth will happen to us; that is when we will begin experiencing eternal joy.

On the day we die all our suffering ends, and we enter eternal joy.

When you realize this truth, how can you be the least bit sad or frightened when your time to die arrives? I honestly cannot wait for my day to die, the day that I will join God, Jesus, and yes, my dad, in eternal life.

Love,
Dad

P.S. – Kids, I am well into my 50s now. And all this time I've been looking for the answer, for the truth, for meaning. The ironic thing is that it was all the time right there waiting for me to discover it. God was waiting patiently for me to come to him. Seeking him always, that is the answer. Living according to his will is the only way to truth. It is truth. Accepting Jesus as our Lord and Savior after repenting for our sins—and then living accordingly—is the only path to truth, meaning, and true happiness.

But God, being rich in mercy, because of the great love with which he loved us, even when we were dead in our trespasses, made us alive together with Christ—by grace you have been saved—and raised us up with him and seated us with him in the heavenly places in Christ Jesus, so that in the coming ages he might show the immeasurable riches of his grace in kindness toward us in Christ Jesus. For by grace you have been saved through faith. And this is not your own doing; it is the gift of God, not a result of works, so that no one may boast. For we are his workmanship, created in Christ Jesus for good works, which God prepared beforehand, that we should walk in them.

Ephesians 2:4-10

Leaving Babylon

Do not love the world or the things in the world. If anyone loves the world, the love of the Father is not in him. For all that is in the world—the desires of the flesh and the desires of the eyes and pride of life—is not from the Father but is from the world. And the world is passing away along with its desires, but whoever does the will of God abides forever.

1 John 2:15-17

BABYLON
Forsaking this World

Their end is destruction, their god is their belly, and they glory in their shame, with minds set on earthly things.

Philippians 3:19

August 2021

Children,

I just turned 55 years old this month, so it feels like a good time to write again. You two kids are all grown up now and succeeding on your own. Alek with your little family started, and Autumn with your career started and college nearly completed. Both of you living on your own and doing well. I've realized that I need to get these letters to you soon; I want you to read them before this world creeps too much into your lives and tries to take over your souls.

Your mom and I have learned in recent years of the futility of trying to live in, and for, this world. And so, as you can probably tell, we've transformed to start living as if we're putting this world behind us.

As you know, we just moved from crowded Florida to a place that feels like we stepped back into the 1980s. Florida was nice, but it was getting overcrowded with people, all of whom appear to live for this world. Even most of the Christians seem to live that way, but I guess that's the case everywhere.

Everything is so much simpler where we are today, in the foothills of the Appalachian Mountains. People are supremely nice and humble, they enjoy simple pleasures, and they truly value family and friends *in person* instead of merely online. I'm sure many people here are on social media, like everywhere else, but you just don't get that sense when you meet them in your daily life. People here truly value relationships and the simple joys of life. Maybe these folks simply have their priorities straight: to keep real relationships ahead of virtual ones. What a concept!

We came here looking for a more slow, innocent lifestyle, and we indeed found it. When you visit us, you'll see what I mean.

Speaking of social media, I finally wised up by following your mom's lead and I've also completely abandoned it. The funny thing is that it only took about a month for me to not miss it any longer. I now find it amusing when I hear about things going on in the virtual world. I honestly love being on the outside of that world, and not even caring to peek in at it. I don't want to know about that world anymore because it's all phony, in my opinion.

The rest of the world sinks deeper and deeper into their obsessions with the virtual world, keeping up with the Joneses, and trying to impress each other online. But your mom and I have decided that we're purely going to live and enjoy each other's company and the people we meet here. I believe that's how life is meant to be lived.

I've also managed to break my only other worldly flaws: being moderately obsessed with sports and politics. I was never nearly as bad as many people, but I still think I was preoccupied with these things more than I should have been. It's nice to now have a *take it or leave it* attitude about both sports and politics. I pretty much only check the headlines of both arenas now. I follow politics only enough to maintain an awareness of what's coming our way, in order to be prepared. And with sports, I like to simply check what teams are doing well, and maybe have a football game on in the background, while I take care of more meaningful things.

It has been a nice change. And while I shouldn't be shocked, I was happily surprised at how much extra time I have available now. Minimizing the importance that social media, sports, and politics have in my life has opened up a lot of free time for more meaningful things.

Those worldly things are such time wasters. Today I realize that my obsessions with being popular on social media, and being consumed with politics and sports, were a big part of why my family grew to hate me back when we lived on Calvary Road.

Take politics, for instance. I've realized that unless you are going to fully dive in and try to make a change in this world via political activities (running for office, starting an organization, making calls to politicians, etc.), there is zero reason anyone should be obsessed with following politics in the news and on social media. People are simply wasting their time if they are just going to obsess and whine and moan about politics. Following all that filth at an obsessive level is not only a huge time waster, but it rots one's soul and turns a person into a miserable pessimist. That was me.

As for sports, it is now my opinion that the only people who should be consumed with sports are those whose kids are playing in the actual games. Sure, sports are a great way to relax and forget about the stress of one's job, etc. But too many sports fans take it far beyond this. People spend hours and hours per week watching sports, following their favorite teams, and obsessing over their fantasy league players.

I once calculated that your average die-hard college and pro football fan probably spends more than 20 hours a week just watching games (college and pro), and who knows how many hours they spend listening to sports talk, watching the highlights, researching fantasy players, etc. And that's only football. How sad. Imagine the kind of projects a person could complete, or goals they could achieve, with an extra 20 hours a week?

And what about Christians who are obsessed sports fans? To them I would ask, "Do you spend 20 hours per week in Christian activities: prayer, Bible study, evangelizing, charity, loving on others?" I pray that you kids take these words to heart and don't ever become obsessed with these kinds of things, like I did.

And as I've cut these time wasters out of my life, I've also eliminated other things out of my life (or never allowed them in) that many people obsess over. People obsess about having the latest gadgets and products, going on the trendiest vacations, and on and on ad nauseam.

On its face, it feels like a wonderful thing that here in the good ol' U.S. of A. we have an outrageous abundance of options in our lives. Options for TV viewing, media devices, social media, and other entertainment options, sports options, etc. We have unlimited options on how to spend our time: vacation options, event options, options in hobbies, and options in leisure activities and other amusements.

I don't view this abundance of options as a blessing, however. Not anymore. I view them as distractors. Of course, it's perfectly fine to have interests and hobbies. But when all these worldly options are merely a means of filling every moment of your life, then that's a problem.

It seems that people can't bear the thought of having a quiet moment in their life, much less, time for God. People, even Christians, succumb to this urge to fill every moment of their lives with activity and things. I think many are trying to fill a God-sized hole in their life that can never be filled with anything but God. Only God can fill that void.

I have fallen short myself from time to time, especially during that terrible span of years on Calvary Road. I got caught up in all the latest worldly trends, and I severely regret it. Today I feel ashamed about that period of my life. I am thankful, though, that I was not more obsessed with the world, or I may have been beyond help.

Today, I love the fact that your mom and I are not the least obsessed with *things*. We are not obsessed with having the latest model cars (obviously, LOL), and in fact we are down to having just one car. We were never tempted by the latest cell phones or technological gadgets like virtual assistants or robot vacuums, the latest home decorating styles, etc. I could go on and on, but you get it.

You see, kids, as my eyes have begun to open to the truth in recent years, I've come to realize that the things in this world are irrelevant. The things that steal our time and the material things that consume our minds and our money, all have zero importance in the grand scheme of things for a Christian.

I think back on all the things that I wrongly focused on throughout my life, and while I mock myself for how naïve I was, I also mourn for all that lost time. Maybe my long, winding path of foolish thinking and misguided priorities was the path required of me, by God, to truly open my eyes and my heart.

As a young idiot, I thought that after high school graduation I could coast through life in comfort. I'm embarrassed now that I ever thought that was the answer to life. I truly was a dumb and immature kid.

Then I thought that partying and adventure, and even partying on an international level, were the answer and a worthy goal in life. It didn't take me long to realize that living for such goals is momentary and fleeting.

When I was in college, I believed that gaining wisdom was the answer. While that was a step in the right direction, I stopped at worldly wisdom and failed to continue searching for the true wisdom that lie in knowing God. Not a wise move, and not the right answer to what life is all about.

While in the Peace Corps I found both love for another person and a love for God's creation, his beautiful Earth. These were steps in the right direction, too, but not nearly the whole answer.

Perhaps not coincidentally, it was coming back to the United States—the world capital of worldly desires—when things quickly spun out of control for me. In my efforts to *fit in* in the world—start a career and family and make life comfortable for that family—I not only lost whatever focus I had on seeking the answer to life, but I forgot that I even had a question!

Luckily for me, it took just three simple men to wake me up and reveal to me the answers to life, and thus the truth.

My two friends—Mike, my homeless friend in Cincinnati, and Wade, the struggling single dad in Paducah—retaught me two important truths that I'd long forgotten from my youth. Those truths are the two great commandments to love God and love others. Plain and simple.

And my dad, in his final days, reminded me that acknowledging that Christ died for my sins and then repenting for those sins, is critical. Because then, living those two great commandments will occur naturally. Dad's life was a reminder that if I live out those great commandments, like he did, my future life with God is secured.

Now that I have the truth in hand, it has become amazingly easy to leave our modern Babylon behind. I have essentially checked out from everything that the rest of the country (and much of the world) is consumed by. I've quit marching to that tune, and instead follow the truth that I now understand.

And not a moment too soon, I would say.

We're right in the middle of the COVID-19 pandemic, as well as extremely ugly political and cultural clashes in our country and across the world. Political forces and the media are hell bent on keeping us at each other's throats, on every topic imaginable. And the hate that people on all sides of the spectrum cling to is growing in magnitude every year.

Real evil seems to be lurking behind all that is going on in recent years. Society is moving toward sin and evil at a rapid rate. Things that would have been unimaginable in my youth are today viewed as ho-hum and common. Things that go against the teachings of the Bible, and the fabric of what our country used to stand for, have taken hold of many Americans.

Making matters worse, I fear that forces are intentionally trying to change our country (and the world, for that matter) into an entirely God-less place. Millions of people seem to hate God simply because they want to be him. They insist that they are God and that they need not answer to anyone for anything. They believe that there is no such thing as sin or evil, and that instead all things are equal.

I think maybe God was preparing me for just this time, and he wants me to also prepare you for tough times ahead. Christians worldwide, I fear, may be in for very rough times ahead. And while this is not new to Christians globally, it would be a new reality for Christians in our country.

And unfortunately, I simply don't know if American Christians are prepared for rough times, for suffering for their beliefs.

Love,
Dad

P.S. – Kids, after many of my own failures and wrong turns, I have finally learned the truth. And now that I see the truth, I've forsaken my own Babylon. I was seeking the answers to life in one false god after another—fun, self-fulfillment, money, stuff, social status, and more. One shiny Babylonian prize after the one before, none of which satisfied my search for truth.

It took me far too many years to realize that the treasures of Babylon are an illusion, and that I should instead travel a different route, a pure and narrow path. Throughout my life I've passed through many neighborhoods of Babylon. That is the best way to describe all those wrong turns and deceptive answers to life—they are merely sleazy streets and neighborhoods of Babylon.

My hope is that you can recognize the false Babylonian gods for what they truly are—worthless idols.

Let those with eyes see and ears hear.

"Do not lay up for yourselves treasures on earth, where moth and rust destroy and where thieves break in and steal, but lay up for yourselves treasures in heaven, where neither moth nor rust destroys and where thieves do not break in and steal. For where your treasure is, there your heart will be also."

Matthew 6:19-21

ZION
Seeking Citizenship Elsewhere

"Enter by the narrow gate. For the gate is wide and the way is easy that leads to destruction, and those who enter by it are many. For the gate is narrow and the way is hard that leads to life, and those who find it are few."

Matthew 7:13-14

August 2022

Kids,

An entire year has passed already since my last letter. My goodness. This is my final letter and message, and then I'll put all of these together and give them to you.

I went back and reread my last letter where I suggest that you leave this world behind, so to speak. To leave behind this materialistic, greedy, self-idolizing, and sinful world. But I suppose I need to clarify what the alternative is, how you should live your life if you're going to forsake the sinful world as we know it.

The Bible talks about entering by the narrow gate, and I like to think of that metaphor more as walking a narrow path through life. This as opposed to a wide path or the wide gate, which represents the broad, easy path that most people in the world walk. The narrow path is difficult to stay on, but it is the path you should strive to live on. This is the path to God.

I came across several Bible passages, with striking imagery, that have stuck in my head in recent years. It comes from Jeremiah chapter 51. It talks about how God intends to destroy Babylon as judgment for its many sins and its attitude of ignoring God. In fact, my version of the Bible titles this chapter "The Utter Destruction of Babylon." Pretty blunt. That chapter also talks about how God's people should forsake Babylon and flee to Zion, God's holy city.

I do think that today's America, and honestly much of the world, fully represents that godless city of old, Babylon. It seems like our country has gotten way off track in an incredibly short span of time. I blame the internet, technology, and social media for much of this. But the greatest blame goes to people simply rejecting, or forgetting, God.

The sinfulness of this world is just unbelievable, as you know, and getting worse every day, every year. I honestly don't see any other course of action for a Christian but to forsake this Babylon. In Philippians chapter 3 the Apostle Paul tells us to focus on eternal life and avoid the deniers of Christ. He says, *"Brothers, join in imitating me, and keep your eyes on those who walk according to the example you have in us. For many, of whom I have often told you and now tell you even with tears, walk as enemies of the cross of Christ. Their end is destruction, their god is their belly, and they glory in their shame, with minds set on earthly things. But our citizenship is in heaven, and from it we await a Savior, the Lord Jesus Christ..."* (*Philippians 3:17-20*).

Our citizenship is in heaven.

That is the key. Walk every day of your life as if you are a foreigner here in this modern-day Babylon. As a true believer, you are a citizen of heaven, and you are only temporarily here in Babylon. Don't let the troubles you have in this life affect you too much, because you need to understand that you truly are here but temporarily.

Walk a narrow path in this life so that you can enter the narrow gate into heaven. Follow the two great commandments and everything else will work out fine. Never let this world hurt you too badly, and never get obsessed with anything in this world.

My greatest warning to you is to not let idols creep in and consume you. And these idols are not little statues of gods like in the Bible. Today's idols include worshipping fun, partying, immoral sex, excessive focus on yourself, love of money, getting a big house, owning a cool new vehicle, and trying to keep up with the Joneses to have all the latest gadgets. Other less obvious idols include obsessing over the many time wasters available to us, many of which I've mentioned already, including social media. The quantity and variety of idols available to us today is unlimited.

I say that these are all modern idols, but I guess many of the same idols were available in days of old. An idol is anything that takes up your time and resources more than the time you spend with God and the time you spend doing his will. We simply have more idols to choose from today.

So, how to live?

That has been my question since that summer of 1984.

I now have the answer nearly 40 years later. I hope after reading my letters you kids will have a much better idea about the answer to life and what truth is, and not have to struggle to find them decades later, like me.

But how to live out that truth is another question. I believe the way to live is simply, humbly, and according to the Bible.

What does that look like?

Well, that can look different for different people. But I will tell you what it looks like for your mom and me. It means living humbly, not feeling like you have to have a new car or the latest cell phone. It also means not getting sucked into social media or getting obsessed with time wasters like sports and politics. I think you both have done this pretty well. In fact, you two kids are much further along than I was at your age. I pray to God that continues.

But an important aspect of living with an eye toward eternity is to really get close to the Lord, spending time with him every day, becoming part of a church community, and volunteering your time and resources (yes, money) to those in need.

You know, when we lived in Florida, everybody on social media acted jealous of me, solely because I lived in Florida. Everyone assumes that Florida is such a fantastic place to live, where life is always a party, you're always at the beach, etc. And that is true for many people.

But do you want to know the truth? The most enjoyable and meaningful times I had in Florida weren't on the beach or at a beach bar. Rather, my favorite time was a two-year stretch where every Saturday morning I volunteered at our church's mobile food pantry. A couple of guys and me directed the traffic weaving through the church parking lot. It was enjoyable because I was able to talk to and joke around with all the people who came to get free groceries.

During the COVID pandemic that meant a lot of people, because a lot of people lost their jobs during that time.

So, yes, that was my favorite thing to do in Florida. Call me weird, but that's what I mean when I tell you that you need to forsake this world and choose the narrow path.

There are a couple of other things that my life includes, which keep me on this narrow path. For several years now I have consistently read at least one chapter of the Bible per day, every day, every week, every month, every year. I try to also read some type of devotional on a daily basis.

All that reading and study really helps you discover the truth and the answers to life, according to the Bible. And not accidentally, all the answers to life's questions actually are in that big old book. Yes, even the answers to life in 2022. Being immersed in the Bible also gives you a much clearer focus in life, not to mention bringing you closer to God.

Walking the narrow path also means, for us at least, giving the full tithe of our income to the church, and another 2-3% to charities that we feel strongly about. And it means giving your time to help those in need around you. That can mean on a purely personal level (e.g., random acts of kindness), or it can mean volunteering with charitable organizations. Honestly, I'm trying to get to a point where I give not only 10% of my income but also at least 10% of my *time* to God through charitable works.

As you read this you may be thinking, "Walking the narrow path seems too hard." To which I would say that embracing the narrow path is just like any other habit that you want to start. At first it is pretty rough and it kinda sucks, I won't lie. But with consistency you can make any habit pretty easy to not only maintain but start enjoying.

Today, I don't even consider all these things to be habits, but rather, just my way of life. And I can honestly say that I love this way of life more than all the other ways of life I've tried before. You, too, will come to love it more than any other way of life, eventually. Why? Because you will know in your heart and mind that it is the most honorable and righteous way to live.

Don't get me wrong, other people will make it hard for you. You must realize that you're going to be ridiculed for walking the narrow path. Your coworkers, friends, and even family members will mock you both to your face and behind your back about the path you have chosen. And that's okay. Honestly, this is as it should be.

The Apostle Paul admits to his friend Timothy, *"Indeed, all who desire to live a godly life in Christ Jesus will be persecuted."* (*2 Timothy:3:12*) And Jesus himself teaches us in his Sermon on the Mount, *"Blessed are those who are persecuted for righteousness' sake, for theirs is the kingdom of heaven. Blessed are you when others revile you and persecute you and utter all kinds of evil against you falsely on my account. Rejoice and be glad, for your reward is great in heaven, for so they persecuted the prophets who were before you."* (*Matthew 5:10-12*)

For your reward is great in heaven!

So you see kids, it is all part of the plan. If you find yourself being mocked and persecuted for your beliefs and your way of life, you will know you are on the right track...the narrow path.

Love,

Dad

P.S. – Let me reiterate: Forsake what everybody else does: idolizing money, fame, stuff, likes, worldly fun, and *living your best life now*. Instead, live simply and humbly, love others, and idolize only God, Jesus, and the Holy Spirit. Keep your life on the narrow path and keep your eye on your citizenship in heaven. You will come to love this way of life, and you will not regret it.

Live for your future citizenship. Look toward eternity, toward Zion.

Live as if forsaking Babylon is the only logical path.

> *We would have healed Babylon, but she was not healed.*
> *Forsake her, and let us go each to his own country, for her*
> *judgment has reached up to heaven and has been lifted up*
> *even to the skies. The Lord has brought about our vindication;*
> *come, let us declare in Zion the work of the Lord our God.*

Jeremiah 51:9-10

EPILOGUE
Lessons in Scarcity

Keep your life free from love of money, and be content with what you have, for he has said, "I will never leave you nor forsake you."

Hebrews 13:5

September 2022

Kids,

You may be wondering how you will be able to forsake this world, and instead walk the narrow path. You may think it's an impossible feat, what I am proposing to you.

With that in mind, I thought I would add the following perspective. Your whole life has been bombarded with advertisements for *stuff* that pop up in front of your eyes all day long. It's not your fault, but the fault of our greedy, consumerist society. People have been programmed to believe that constant consumption of material goods and fun is the only way to live.

It isn't.

In fact, human beings can survive just fine with a pretty significant level of scarcity.

Your mom and I had a friend, Kevin, who lived in a nearby town during our time in the Peace Corps in Paraguay. His tour was about to end when ours was only getting started. One day he was telling us his stories and tips on how to survive the life we were just beginning. He described Peace Corps life very simply: "It's a lot like camping, but for two years straight."

Kevin nailed it with that description.

Camping is not far from the truth. Yes, we did have a house to live in, but not anything like you find in the U.S. today, or even 30, 50, 70 years ago. I'll start from the top. Our house had ceramic shingles, which you could see from the inside as easily as from the outside of the house. In other words, no ceilings, only rafters and shingles. The walls were comprised of cheap, chalky stucco on equally cheap brick. The floors consisted of uneven brick, which always needed to be swept of sand and dirt. We lived with this for two years.

Our kitchen was, well, both outdoors and indoors. Our only sink was out back; think of a wash basin like people have next to their washer/dryer. That served as the kitchen sink and our clothes washer (yes, washing clothes by hand, in cold water). We didn't have a stove, oven, or microwave. Rather, we had a miniature propane tank with a flame shooting out the top, and we rigged a way to set pots and pans on it to cook. We had no refrigerator, only a cooler that we refilled with ice every couple of days. Needless to say, we had to grocery shop (if you can call it that) every few days…for two years.

We had no air conditioning of any sort, just a couple of small fans.

And Paraguay gets very hot in the summer…think Caribbean heat. Our furniture was very meager: a simple double bed, a couple sets of folding wooden chairs and tables, and a few other things we could use to hang our clothes and kitchen supplies. We did have a small cassette radio, and a decent collection of cassette tapes that we each brought with us from the U.S. That was our musical enjoyment.

No TV, no phone, no video games, and computers and cell phones weren't even a thing yet. This was the early 1990s. If we wanted to call someone back home, we had to walk up to the local phone company building and wait for an available booth. And then, if you could get through to who you wanted to call, you often heard a terrible echo during the conversation. No one could call us, however. How could they? We wouldn't know that they were trying to call us at the phone company…for two years.

Our diet was pretty healthy. We didn't trust buying the local beef (one look at the fly-infested butcher's shop and you'd agree). For meat, I think we only bought rotisserie-style chicken or had canned tuna or canned chicken. We had a nice garden for vegetables, and we could usually trust the produce in our town's market. The meals I remember the most were green salad, potato salad, macaroni salad, and grilled cheese with chives. And lots of rice and pasta.

Oh, and popcorn. My fondest memory (ha, ha) was of your mom sitting on the porch steps picking through every corn kernel before popping it. Why? Because she wanted to throw out the kernels that had evidence of being eaten by bugs, or with bugs still in them. That's why.

I almost forgot the best part (and by *best* I only mean the best way to paint this picture of scarcity). We had an outhouse for a bathroom. That sounds terrible, I know, but your mom did make a nice toilet seat—a fabric-covered wooden crate—for us to sit on. At one point we had a bit of trouble, though, as a possum was trying to take over the outhouse as his own. Imagine having to clear your bathroom of possum before you could *comfortably* take a seat...for two years.

Our shower was slightly better (except in the winter). The shower was outdoors, like the outhouse. We'd take our towel and change of clothes to the shower, about ten yards out back. Picture a little brick shower stall, with a gap all around the top at about above eye level, and a curtain for a door. This was fine most of the year, but we had no hot water. So, when winter temperatures got down to about 40 degrees Fahrenheit, well, let's just say that your mom opted for warm sponge baths in the house. I was much braver: I waited until the warmest time of the day to take a one-minute ice-cold shower.

As far as transportation, we had three options: walk, ride a bike, or hop on the rickety, disgusting school-type buses filled with sweaty passengers and farm animals. The scarcity of paved roads meant that these bus rides often left you nauseous...for two years.

I'm currently reading John Steinbeck's *The Grapes of Wrath*. It's funny, the folks in that story, set in the late 1930s United States, had it about as good as we did. That's rather amazing now that I think of it. In many ways we were living like the Joad family of the 1930s...for two years.

Upon enlisting for the Peace Corps, I learned that on average, 25% of Peace Corps volunteers quit before finishing their two-year tours. I guess the culture shock is too much for them. That number may surprise you. But the number that is more shocking, if we're being honest, is the other 75%. Yes, 75% of American volunteers can indeed handle the kind of culture shock I've just described. Quite amazing, really.

Why do I tell you all of this? Not to gain pity. I tell you this to make the point that the human body and mind can put up with an awful lot. I realize that in the 1990s your mom and I didn't have all the same comforts of today, but the 1990s were a lot more advanced than the 1930s. We were able to give all that up, almost overnight. We volunteered to live like that, and we not only survived but we enjoyed it. Yes, we complained, but certainly not more than today's Americans complain about their standard of living.

We create in our minds the conditions we *think* we can or cannot put up with.

If I went back to Paraguay today, I would not be surprised if many of those people still live in the same way. I've seen enough images and videos taken by Christian missionaries and others to know that in many countries around the world, this is how a large percentage of the world still lives.

In fact, when your mom and I went on a cruise for our 25th wedding anniversary about five years ago, we saw extreme scarcity all over again. On two of the cruise's day trips, we went into the interior of both Honduras and Belize. Let's just say that we had flashbacks of Paraguay 1992.

So yes, even today, life in many countries looks just like 1990s Paraguay, which is much like 1930s America.

Yet here at home, if a hurricane or tornado knocks our power out for a couple of days, we act like Armageddon has arrived. Everything is relative. Many people around the world live with little or no power every day.

Let's go even further and consider absolute scarcity and need. Think of the vast degrees of what the human body, mind, and soul can put up with to survive. If you know your history at all, you learned about the Holocaust, the Soviet gulags, and countless other histories of utter misery, starvation, and scarcity. And while millions did not survive those conditions, many other millions did. And closer to home, people suffered through and survived the Great Depression and the Dust Bowl less than 100 years ago.

But today, if the local Starbucks, Chick-Fil-A, or Target store closes down, we think we'll surely perish. Meanwhile, millions around the world barely have a local corner store for purchasing all their needs.

It is as if the human body, soul, and mind are always mindful that they came into this world with nothing, and they will leave this world with just as much. We humans can be pretty tough when we need to be. Regrettably, we haven't needed to be tough in a long, long time in this country.

I'm pretty sure that we in the U.S. are the ones who are the outliers, the exception to the norm in this world. The endless supply of material goods, the mind-boggling gadgets, and ever-new technological widgets at our disposal. While our society is cluttered with material junk, our minds are cluttered with even more garbage. We bombard our minds with entertainment, products, sports, politics, faux cultural nonsense, memes and Gifs, pointless video clips, more products, trivial thoughts, empty ideas, and worldly hopes and dreams.

Our options for consuming food, drink, drugs, and alcohol are endless. Even our time is filled to the nth degree with duties, chores, and society-demanding activities.

Yeah, I'm fairly sure that from a global perspective, we are the oddballs. We fill our lives with stuff and things just because we can, with no thought as to the value of those things.

One amazing yet simple reality is that much of those things we think we *can't live without* haven't even been around all that long. I'll give you a few examples. You know these products, but you may not realize how relatively new they are.

Electric vacuum cleaners have only been in common use for about 100 years, yet today we act as if we can't survive without our robotic vacuum assistant. The first refrigerators for the home have also only been around for about 100 years. And somehow…somehow people survived before their arrival.

The automatic drip coffee maker didn't become common until the 1970s. God forbid we be forced to make coffee in a more primitive fashion. During our Paraguay years, we made our daily coffee by placing a handkerchief inside of a kitchen strainer, then scooped in the coffee grounds and carefully poured hot water overtop…for two years.

Appliances like electric dishwashers and washers and dryers for clothes weren't in the common family's home until the 1950s or later. That's merely 70 years ago. Central air conditioning wasn't a thing until the 1950s, and even then, only for the wealthy. Microwave ovens weren't common in homes until the late 1980s. Can you imagine?

I spent my childhood without either a microwave oven or any sort of air conditioning. People today would think they had been tossed in a torture chamber, not having those two things.

As for our most modern technological conveniences, those have an even shorter history. I think the internet and people having their own personal computers wasn't common until the mid-1990s. That's barely 25 years ago.

The first common video game system was Nintendo, which didn't come out until the mid-1980s. Listening to music on the go? It wasn't a thing until 1979 when the now-lame Sony Walkman arrived. (We thought it was the coolest thing on the planet at the time.) Smartphones didn't arrive until the early 2000s, and the iPhone in 2007. Today these are so common that the unenlightened probably believe they've been around forever.

And last but not least, social media and streaming TV. Those weren't common until the early- and mid-2000s. As for the companies we love (or hate), Amazon didn't arrive until the mid-1990s, Google a few years later, and YouTube didn't show up until the mid-2000s.

Remarkable, really, when you consider how all these things are deemed indispensable, but which haven't even been around all that long. How in the world did we function without them?

Well, we did, and I and many others like me are starting to realize that we were probably doing better as a society without them. At least maybe without social media and smartphones.

Sure, I will admit that life was less convenient without these modern technologies, but it sure was more innocent and authentic.

Your mom and I have been moving into a time of reading more—books, devotionals, and historical or otherwise educational content—and spending less time with politics, news and popular media, and social media. As we've started doing that, your mom reminded me of something very beautiful.

She said that she misses how we used to read every night in bed together in Paraguay, and how enjoyable, peaceful, and fulfilling that time was. I even used to read various short stories and the Bible to your mom, which she especially enjoyed.

I honestly think that our Peace Corps years were the most gratifying times of our lives. Those memories of our life of scarcity, and the enjoyment of rare treats when we found them, gave us a great deal of appreciation. Appreciation not for stuff but for the simple blessings God provides.

That reminds me of a quote that has formed in my head over the past few years, and I contemplate it often:

> "Throughout my life, I have always been the
> closest to God, and to the truth, when I had
> the least, when my life was the simplest."

I think that's how I've been able to finally see the truth, the truth that I need to focus on God and eternity above all else. I started removing the clutter from my mind and from my life overall. It turns out that the best way to find the truth is to forsake all the trappings of this world, to strip away as much of this false world as possible, and to instead choose scarcity. Then you can see the truth that was there all along, hidden behind all the junk.

You see, kids, when you choose scarcity as a way of life, it's not truly scarcity. Rather, it's the greatest blessing of all. If you choose to live *without*, you aren't lacking anything because you've chosen that lifestyle. You aren't poor at all. You may appear poor to others, but you and God know otherwise.

Love,
Dad

P.S. – Kids, it's not impossible to embrace the simple, honorable lifestyle. It does take time. But you can do it bit by bit, by trading things. What do I mean by that? Trade a little bit of time spent watching TV for time reading the Bible. Trade some time scrolling through social media with time spent talking to and praying to God. Trade some of the money you spend on worthless junk on Amazon and give it to a worthy cause. Trade some of the time you waste on who knows what for time volunteering to help the needy.

If you can do this bit by bit, month after month, and then year after year, pretty soon you will be living a life of scarcity. And these will be the best years of your life.

"Look at the birds of the air: they neither sow nor reap nor gather into barns, and yet your heavenly Father feeds them. Are you not of more value than they? And which of you by being anxious can add a single hour to his span of life? And why are you anxious about clothing? Consider the lilies of the field, how they grow: they neither toil nor spin, yet I tell you, even Solomon in all his glory was not arrayed like one of these. But if God so clothes the grass of the field, which today is alive and tomorrow is thrown into the oven, will he not much more clothe you, O you of little faith? Therefore do not be anxious, saying, 'What shall we eat?' or 'What shall we drink?' or 'What shall we wear?' For the Gentiles seek after all these things, and your heavenly Father knows that you need them all. But seek first the kingdom of God and his righteousness, and all these things will be added to you."

Matthew 6:26-33

You shall love the Lord your God with all your heart and with all your soul and with all your might. And these words that I command you today shall be on your heart. You shall teach them diligently to your children, and shall talk of them when you sit in your house, and when you walk by the way, and when you lie down, and when you rise.

Deuteronomy 6:5-7

Made in the USA
Columbia, SC
20 February 2023